Creating Your Library Brand

Communicating Your Relevance and Value to Your Patrons

Elisabeth Doucett

American Library Association
Chicago   2008

Elisabeth Doucett is director of the Curtis Memorial Library in Brunswick, Maine. Formerly, she was assistant director of the Lucius Beebe Memorial Library in Wakefield, Massachusetts. She has a master's in library science from Simmons College and an MBA in marketing from the J. L. Kellogg Graduate School of Management at Northwestern University. Her strategy and marketing proficiencies were developed over more than a decade spent in the consumer packaged goods industry as a marketing director at Quaker Oats and Dunkin' Donuts and as a brand manager at Kraft Foods in the Maxwell House Coffee Division.

The paper used in this publication meets the minimum requirements of American National Standard for Information Sciences—Permanence of Paper for Printed Library Materials, ANSI Z39.48-1992. ∞

Library of Congress Cataloging-in-Publication Data
Doucett, Elisabeth.
    Creating your library brand : communicating your relevance and value to your patrons / Elisabeth Doucett.
        p. cm.
    Includes index.
    ISBN-13: 978-0-8389-0962-1 (alk. paper)
    ISBN-10: 0-8389-0962-0 (alk. paper)
    1. Libraries—Marketing. 2. Branding (Marketing) I. Title.
Z716.3.D68 2008
659.1902—dc22   2008000983

ISBN-13: 978-0-8389-0962-1

Printed in the United States of America
12   11   10   09   08   5   4   3   2   1

To my husband, who never doubted for a minute
that I could write a book

Contents

■ ■ ■ ■ ■ ■ ■ ■ ■ ■ ■ ■ ■ ■ ■

Preface

■ ■ ■ ■ ■ ■ ■ ■ ■ ■ ■ ■ ■

I became a full-fledged librarian three years ago when I graduated from Simmons College with a masters in library science. At forty-six years old I was starting a new career. After receiving an MBA in marketing from Northwestern University's Kellogg Graduate School of Management, I had spent the next fifteen years in business. My career involved marketing for and consulting to large companies (Kraft Foods, Quaker Oats, Dunkin' Donuts) that manufactured food products for consumers.

I loved marketing as a profession. It challenges you every day to find a better way of connecting with potential consumers, deciphering what they want from your products, and then delivering what is desired. After many years of being involved in marketing, however, I wanted to reenergize my work involvement and I was interested in exploring other professional directions. I decided that my objectives were to do something I could feel passionate about, to continue using my relevant business experience, and to be involved in an organization that was mission driven rather than profit driven. After much networking, researching, and interviewing about different career opportunities, I decided to go back to school to study library science. Librarianship fit all my goals—I love books and libraries; the profession was completely new for me; and I could work in a public library, which is about as mission driven an organization as exists today. I went to Simmons College in Boston and focused on public libraries. After graduation I became the assistant director of the Lucius Beebe Memorial Library in Wakefield, Massachusetts.

As I started in this new position, I was invigorated by developing new aptitudes and by having a social focus in place of a profit focus. Unexpectedly I found that my business skills could continue to be very useful in the library environment, particularly my skills in marketing.

Over the past five to eight years, libraries have endured a period of intense transition and evolution. The public library used to be one of the primary sources (and sometimes the only source) of information and entertainment in a community. People who grew up prior to World War II went to the library as a matter of course for books, newspapers, and magazines. The prewar and baby-boomer generations used the library as part of their daily routine, to do their homework after school and to do research for school papers.

Once use of the Internet dramatically increased in the late 1990s, however, the library could no longer remain a world unto itself. Information and entertainment come from multiple sources in an immense variety of formats, and new technologies are commonplace. Libraries now vie with the Internet, multifunction cell phones, bookstores, Netflix, Amazon.com, movie theaters, and many, many other competitors for the attention and involvement of their patrons. In the past libraries never had to explain and defend their relevance. They were an accepted and established part of most American communities. Funding for the local public library was generally exempt from struggles over municipal budgets, and colleges and universities took great pride in having outstanding libraries as showcases on their campuses.

Now everything is changing. People have more and more demands on their time. They work more, sleep less, and exercise less, and no one ever seems to have enough time for extra activities like trips to the library. Individuals are joining fewer and fewer civic organizations, making it more difficult to find volunteer support for community institutions. Municipalities are under constant pressure to reduce taxes and find ways to spend less money. Today, these restrictions apply every bit as much to the public library as to the local department of public works. Many students are perfectly happy to fill all of their information needs from the Internet and can go through four years of college without ever entering their campus library. Younger people frequently are not interested in reading books. Because libraries equal books in their minds, they see no value in libraries. The common refrain among all age groups is "I can find everything I need for free on the Internet."

In the midst of all of this change, libraries are struggling to find their new place in the information universe and then to articulate what that place is to existing and potential library users. In the new competitive environment in which they find themselves, libraries can no longer expect that they will automatically maintain their current users and also bring in the next generation of users. They are in need of a tool that will help customers view their local library as a preferred source for the services that library provides. The perfect tool to enable this association is branding.

Branding is a component of the marketing process. It defines to whom you want to talk about your product (and by product I mean product or service—libraries offer both), articulates a clear message about what makes your product unique and meaningful, and conveys that information in a method that captures the potential customer's attention and encourages him to action.

Branding helps libraries develop a laser-sharp message about the role they play in their communities, and it helps them ensure that the message is delivered in a way that will have a measurable impact on potential users. It should be noted that a library's branding message is related to but not the same as a library's mission statement. A mission statement is an articulation of why an organization exists and includes its goals, aspirations, and values. It is generally an internal strategic document, meant to act as a guide that tells the organization how it should operate. A library's branding statement is more externally focused. It is meant to convey the library's role to its public in terms that are meaningful and relevant to that public.

The Lucius Beebe Memorial Library in Wakefield, Massachusetts, is a perfect case study for the need to develop a branding message. The library had a clear mission statement. It did a wonderful job of promoting specific events, activities, and services. However, when I asked staff and members of the community what made the library unique, I received many different answers, none of which was consistent with the others or with the library's mission. Although the library had a very good logo, it had not determined a way to use that logo consistently to maximize recognition. Therefore, with the support of my library director, I initiated a branding process that would help the library clarify its story and give it a brand look that would help convey that story quickly and effectively.

Initially I thought branding for a library would be very similar to the process I had used many times in the corporate world. Although the basic elements were the same, they needed to be tweaked and adjusted for the realities of a public library. The staff at most libraries have very specific job responsibilities that take up most of their time. It is rare that they have time to think about more strategic questions such as, "What role should the library play in the community?" There is never enough money in a public library to do extra projects such as developing interesting and intriguing branding materials. Yet a brand message and design are two of the most important elements of communication that a library can have. They get ignored or put on the back burner because no one has the time or energy to figure out how to do this work within the library's constraints.

As I took my library through a branding process, I kept in mind how this work could be done within the restrictions that all libraries face in terms of time and resources. Practicality became my focus. To make sure that I avoided work that was unnecessary, my first step was always to question why I was doing a specific component of branding. I tried to set up the work that needed to be done so that the process was streamlined and could be executed quickly before getting staff involved. To minimize funding requests for professional design work, I tried to find ways of getting the work done with no spending. Also, I continuously challenged myself to find methods of explaining branding in a simple, straightforward way that eliminated marketing jargon. (Librarians are not the only ones who depend a great deal on their own special language.) This helped make the branding process easily accessible to anyone, not just to people with a background in marketing.

The result was the development of a very practical branding process for the library that was both efficient and effective in terms of the time, energy, and investment needed to execute it. This book is a compilation of that work. Any public library can adapt this process to achieve success in the new competitive entertainment and information environment.

 Suggestion for Success

Do not be afraid of branding

You do not need to be a brain surgeon to do branding (or marketing). Once you understand the basics, it is mostly a case of trusting your own instincts about what is right for your library. Just remember, if something does not seem right, it probably is wrong. Listen to your intuition. Also, before you start any branding project spend some time looking at what other libraries have done. You can teach yourself a great deal by reviewing others' work and deciding for yourself what you do and do not like about what they have done.

How to Use This Book

■ ■ ■ ■ ■ ■ ■ ■ ■ ■ ■ ■ ■

As I started writing this book, I thought it was important to develop guidelines that people could dip into on an as-needed basis. Many libraries have done some branding and may already have a logo or even a full branding process. Therefore, they do not need to start at chapter 1 and read the entire book through to the end. A book on branding is more useful to libraries that have done some branding if the reader can identify where she is in the branding process, start at that chapter, and then go forward from there. Consequently, each chapter in this book is meant to be a stand-alone segment. Individuals may read chapters as their interests and needs dictate.

In an additional effort to make this book practical, I have included an exercise at the end of each chapter to help put the content in a realistic context. In many cases these are exercises that I have worked through with library staff as part of a branding process. Based on staff feedback, changes were made to ensure the exercises are as effective as possible. Throughout the book you will also find tips, suggestions for success, and answers to frequently asked questions to help you get the work done within the constraints that all of us in libraries face.

The table below is meant to help in this process. It lays out a plan for meetings and exercises that will take a team through the entire branding process. It can act as a guide to help the project leader or library director understand what is involved in a branding project and what activities are needed to implement branding in a library. Each project leader should, however, create a customized plan, depending on who is involved and what needs to be achieved. Also, if a library hires an outside consultant to help with branding, the process will change based on the degree of help and input provided by the consultant.

By the end of this book, no matter how new you are to branding, you will have a good, basic understanding of what branding is; why it can be very useful to your library; and how you can develop a brand for your library, put it into use, and then evaluate its ultimate success. The end result should be better marketing for your library and more patrons walking through your door.

Sample Project Plan

Project activity	How to do the activity	Who should do the activity	Exercises to complete
Educate yourself about branding—what it is and why it is important for libraries	Read entire book but particularly chapters 1–4 and case studies in appendix A	Project leader or library director	Exercise, chapter 1 Read, be familiar with, and be able to lead all exercises in chapters 1–3
Identify who will be on your Core Team, your Checkpoint Team, and your Support Team	Read chapter 3	Project leader or library director	Exercise, chapter 3
Update Checkpoint Team and Support Team		Project leader or library director	
Understand the role of outside help in the branding process and determine if/how you will use it as part of your branding project	Read chapter 9	Project leader or library director	Exercise, chapter 9
Take your Core Team through a basic training process: (1) assign reading, (2) meet twice to go through exercises	Have team read chapters 1–4, and case studies in appendix A	Core Team and project leader	Exercise, chapter 1 Exercise, chapter 2 Exercise, chapter 3 Exercise, chapter 4
Collect materials for brand audit; have Core Team meet to do brand-audit exercise	Have team members read chapter 5, assign responsibilities to team members, collect materials, and, as a team, do chapter 5 exercise	Core Team, project leader, outside help	Exercise, chapter 5
Take staff and board through brand-audit exercise in chapter 5	Have staff and board read chapter 5 and do chapter 5 exercise	Staff, board, project leader	Exercise, chapter 5
Summarize learning from brand audit; determine which elements of branding (message, design) need focus	Review learning from audit and summarize; share with Core Team after brand-audit session	Project manager or library director	

Project activity	How to do the activity	Who should do the activity	Exercises to complete
Develop brand message and tagline	Core Team and project manager read chapter 6 and do the work identified in the chapter	Project manager and Core Team	Exercise, chapter 6
Develop brand image or logo	Core Team and project manager read chapter 7 and do the work identified in the chapter	Project manager and Core Team	Project manager completes exercise, chapter 7
Update Checkpoint Team and Support Team		Project leader or library director	
Develop brand editorial standards and brand design standards; choose a brand advocate	Core Team and project manager read chapter 8 and do the work identified in the chapter	Project manager and Core Team	Project manager completes exercise, chapter 8
Share progress to date with library governing body		Project manager	
Develop transition plan for implementing use of new branding materials		Project manager	See chapter 8
Develop and implement process for evaluating library brand	Core Team and project manager read chapter 10	Project manager in consultation with Core Team	Project manager completes exercise, chapter 10
Develop marketing plan	Project manager rereads chapter 8	Project manager	Project manager follows process in chapter 8
Finalize branding training	Core Team reads chapters 11–13	Project manager and Core Team	Core Team does exercises, chapters 11–13

▪1▪ Defining Marketing and Branding

One of the questions librarians often ask me is, "What are marketing and branding and how do they relate to each other?" *Marketing* is a term used by librarians to mean many different things and therefore has become confusing. *Branding* is a term that is just coming into use in libraries and as a result, very few librarians have a clear understanding of what it means and how it is different from marketing. Therefore, this chapter will focus on defining marketing and branding and identifying how they relate to each other in the library environment. The objective is to establish a common vocabulary and language that can be used throughout the rest of this book.

At its simplest level, marketing is the process of (1) identifying the potential audience that you want to hear your library's story, (2) developing that story so that those potential users understand what makes your library unique and why they will find it interesting, and (3) developing ways of telling the story that will intrigue those users and attract their attention (see figure 1).

Figure 1 What is marketing? Marketing at its simplest level

The first part of the marketing process (identifying who you want to hear the library's story [the audience] and then developing the story) is planning that is done before any actual marketing is put into motion. Therefore, it is called *marketing strategy* (*strategy* being defined as a series of plans developed to achieve a specific goal). The results of the second part of the process (developing and implementing tools to tell the story in a compelling manner) are referred to as *marketing tactics*—actions taken to publicize a product in the marketplace (see figure 2). The following sections offer brief summaries of each of the components of marketing strategy and marketing tactics, and thus provide an overview of the entire marketing process. More information about each component can be found in any book about the marketing process within the general business literature.

Marketing Strategy

The elements of marketing strategy include setting objectives for marketing, identifying who might want to use the library (segmenting), defining those to whom the library's story is going to be told (targeting), defining the library's story (branding), and doing market research to test assumptions about the relevance of the library's story.

Setting Objectives

As in any other strategic process it is important to set objectives, or goals, for the marketing process. Objectives identify what you want to have happen as

Figure 2 Marketing strategy and tactics: How marketing strategy and tactics work together

a result of the entire marketing process. Most libraries pursue one of three marketing objectives: (1) to bring new users into the library, (2) to have existing users come to the library more often, or (3) to do both—bring in new users and have existing users come more often. Each of these objectives will require a different set of marketing tools. Hence, it is crucial to define clearly which one your library wants most to achieve. To be able to measure your success you will also need to make sure that your objective is quantifiable—for example, "to increase the number of new library users by 10 percent over the course of one fiscal year."

Segmenting

To segment your market, you need to identify the total universe of individuals who might use your product, such as all existing library users in the city of Brunswick, and then break that universe into smaller segments, such as mothers with kids under the age of five, that you can study to understand if they might be interested in your product. Segmenting may be done in many different ways. Demographic segmenting is the identification of fairly large groups by demographic factors such as age, gender, income, or geographic location. Groups may also be segmented by shared interests (iPod owners, marathoners, artists). Marketers use segmenting because it helps them gain a more detailed understanding of smaller groups that have something in common. The more detailed understanding in turn helps them decide if they want to try to sell their product to that specific group.

Branding

Branding is one component of marketing strategy. Branding is the process of defining a library's story, distilling that into one short, appealing sentence that tells the whole story, and then visually conveying the story via the library's logo and other branding elements.

 Frequently Asked Question

What is a brand?

Technically, a brand is a mark, or logo, combined with specific colors and fonts that identifies a particular product or service to potential users. More generally, a brand is shorthand for the story that an organization wants to tell potential users about how it can meet a need in their lives.

But what is the *story*? A library's story is the articulation of the role it plays or wants to play in its community. To create a powerful story, the library needs to identify a role that no one else can duplicate. The story is meant to inform anyone considering using the library about what makes it special and worth visiting. The story can be about the details of the library (great customer service, a large collection, a beautiful building), or it can be about the needs that the library could fill in the lives of its patrons. The story might be that the library is a place where a community connects and comes together. It might be the intellectual center of a small town. It could be the tool that parents use to give their kids a head start in life. It could be the center of campus life for a college or a place where a student can feel part of a community at a large university. Any one of these stories would be compelling to people thinking of using the library. They are powerful definitions of what makes the library relevant and important in its community.

It is imperative to remember that as a library develops its story, it should check back with its patrons and potential users to make sure that its story is not only unique but also relevant and meaningful. It is great to say that a library has the largest serials collection in the county, but if potential users do not care about serials, then that story has no relevance and will not help make the library attractive. A meaningful story will motivate potential patrons to come to the library because they are seeking what the library provides. Chapter 6 offers tools to help a library define its special story and then evaluate the relevance of that story.

Having a clear, compelling story is essential to a library's marketing efforts, but equally critical is the library brand look, that is, the visual representation of the library and its story. The look is seen in the library's logo and its colors, specific typefaces that might be used in written publications, pictures of the library building, library cards, name tags worn by staff—any visual representation of the library and its services. The look should support the library's story. This means that if a library story is about the innovation and excitement to be found there, the look cannot be presented in dull colors coupled with a sedate logo and stodgy typesetting. The story and the look must work together. When they do, they become powerful tools that quickly convey a great deal of information to current and potential users. Consistent use of the same typography also can trigger memory, thereby helping people remember and quickly recognize written materials from the library.

It is important to understand that a logo and a brand are not the same thing. A logo is one piece of a brand, albeit the most important piece. A logo is a visual shortcut that identifies an organization, sometimes by using the organization's name (think of the Dunkin' Donuts logo), sometimes by using visual imagery that relates to the organization (think of the Nike swoosh).

A brand comprises many elements in addition to a logo. A brand is made up of the logo, the brand's colors, the typeface used when spelling out the brand name, the brand tagline (Lucius Beebe Memorial Library: Where Wakefield Connects), signage inside and outside the library, name tags that library staff wear, and library cards. A brand is also made up of any experience that an individual might have with the organization. This includes interactions with staff, perceptions of materials in the library, and even simple things such as the availability of parking near the library. All of those things make up a library brand.

Targeting

One of the first phrases that you will hear as you start to become familiar with branding is *target audience*. A target audience is a specific group of people that you want to hear and respond to your branding message. If you were marketing a product (like a new soap or a new car), the whole world would essentially be your potential audience. However, you know that you cannot talk to everyone because you do not have the money to do that much marketing. Consequently, you want your message to be heard by the audience most likely to be interested in your product and be moved to buy it after hearing your advertising. That would be your target audience. By defining a group that will be the focus of your marketing, you can make sure that your message is meaningful and relevant, that it is couched in language your audience will understand, and that it is presented in a place where they are likely to hear it.

Some may wonder how targeting applies to libraries and if libraries need to identify a target audience before they start their branding work. My perspective is that targeting can be a very useful tool for libraries as they develop their message. In the past most libraries tried to craft a message that would get people who had never used the library to try it out, and they just assumed that current patrons would continue to use the library. Today more libraries are understanding that they need to maintain a constant dialogue with their existing users even while they continue to talk with new, potential users. Consequently they have redefined their target audience (and revised their brand message) to encompass this expanded group of both current users and nonusers.

However, some libraries have decided that with limited resources, it is not worth spending the majority of their marketing time and energy getting new users in the door. Rather, they now focus their resources on making sure they are meeting the needs of their current patrons and hope that by doing so they will increase that group's satisfaction and use of the library. Libraries follow different targeting strategies, and those differences have an impact on how they approach their branding.

To identify the best target audience for your library, you need to start by honestly assessing your current library users. Consider the following questions:

- If you are a public library, what percentage of your community has library cards? Who uses your virtual library and for what purposes?
- If you are an academic library, what percentage of students use the library, either virtually or by taking books out?
- Does your community support your library? How do you know—through financial support, through feedback you get from community surveys, or through some other mechanism?
- Is your community aware of the services offered by your library? Again, how do you obtain that information?

Bottom line, through these questions you are trying to understand how much support and use your library receives. If you already have a very strong base of support, then you can probably afford to focus your branding and marketing efforts on current library users such as moms with kids, teenagers, and senior citizens. In this situation you might focus on reinforcing what library users already know about your library—for example, that it is the center of the community and provides learning and connection for people of all ages. If your levels of support and nonsupport are about equal, you probably need to talk to both users and nonusers if you hope to increase your overall library usage because the current group of users is not large enough. If your library has very low support in your community, then you are probably going to focus the majority of your energy on nonusers, demonstrating to them how and why the library is important and why it matters in your community. Your objective in this case is to bring more users into the library.

Market Research

Market research is an important component of any branding or marketing effort. I always say that market research is your library's opportunity to have a dialogue with a large number of your users. You would probably prefer to have that conversation one-on-one if you could. However, that is never possible, so market research is the next best option. Today, market research encompasses a huge number of tools, including interviews, focus groups, surveys, computer analytics—the list goes on and on. The objective of market research is to conduct a "conversation" with a specific group of consumers that will reveal their thoughts about a product or a service. This helps a library (or a company) determine which marketing strategies and tactics make sense to and are likely to have an impact on potential customers.

Marketing Tactics

Marketing tactics are, by and large, more familiar to librarians than marketing strategy. Promotion, advertising, direct marketing, public relations, and sales are all marketing tactics.

Promotion

A promotion is any effort that an organization engages in to develop awareness about a specific activity. A promotion can be as simple as printing out a flyer about a speaker at the library and putting it on a community bulletin board or as complicated as conducting a citywide campaign to ensure that all citizens obtain a library card. Both are meant to increase public knowledge about a library activity. Libraries are generally well aware of promotions and understand how they can be used to increase awareness about specific events.

Advertising

Advertising is the action of talking directly to possible users of your product to tell them how that product can fulfill a need in their lives. In the United States most of us are exposed to tremendous amounts of advertising on a daily basis, so we understand it well. However, because advertising, whether in print, via television or radio, or on the Internet, tends to be expensive, most libraries do not engage in much of it. Also, broadscale advertising (television in particular) aims to address a large percentage of the population, whereas libraries are typically more interested in talking with smaller subsets.

Direct Marketing

Direct marketing includes any form of communication (mail, Internet) that offers goods or services directly to consumers. Libraries tend not to do much direct marketing because it is generally seen as intrusive to send specific offers to library users and because there are not many situations in which specific offers would be appropriate.

Public Relations

Public relations (PR) is any activity that results in a third-party mention of your product or service. Generally the third party is a newspaper or magazine to which you have sent a story idea and that has followed up with a free article about your product or service or something happening at your organization. Libraries are generally quite good at public relations and understand how to use it to get free promotion of their activities.

Sales

The notion of sales is often viewed with distrust in the nonprofit environment. It brings to mind pictures of sleazy used-car salesmen pitching their product. In fact, sales is simply the process of matching a buyer and a seller. People who are talented at sales will not try to force a product on you that you do not want. Instead, their job is to understand what you want and then offer you an appropriate product or service. Sales does not play a huge role in the marketing of libraries, but it is useful to understand how it contributes to marketing in general.

The Complete Marketing Process

All the components of marketing strategy and marketing tactics together make up the complete marketing process (figure 3). Many library staff already use some marketing tactics. Promoting special programs, lectures, or events is something most libraries know how to do well. Libraries understand that unless the community is aware of an event, attendance will not be high enough to warrant the effort on the library's part. Public relations is also an activity that many libraries understand and execute; they get free publicity by sending out information on library programs and activities.

However, what is frequently missing from libraries' marketing efforts is a cohesive strategy based on clearly defined objectives and systematic segmenting, targeting, branding, and market research. Although marketing tactics may be implemented without a marketing strategy, and in libraries they often are, such efforts are highly likely to end up being disjointed or ineffective. Strategy can be thought of as a blueprint. A blueprint provides a contractor with a clear goal and shows what needs to be done to get a house built and to ensure that each room serves the purpose for which it is designed. It makes sure that subcontractors are all working toward the same end and that no one will build a ranch if a colonial is desired. Similarly, a marketing strategy sets a clear direction for everyone in the library, making sure that all tactics are designed to work toward the same goals.

Today, everyone leads a fast-paced life. That is one reason why brands have become ubiquitous. Well-known brands tell their stories quickly and effectively. Their messages are compelling and relevant, and their look is interesting and attention catching. A library's use of branding allows possible users to get fast, accurate information about the library's services without working too hard. It identifies what the library provides to its users *that they cannot get anywhere else.*

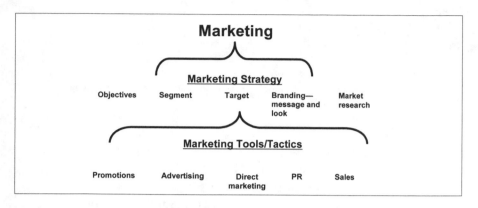

Figure 3 The marketing mix: All the elements of marketing

Having a consistent message and look that emphasize a library's uniqueness also ensures that all tactical marketing activities, such as promotions and public relations, follow a coherent and consistent approach. It helps everyone in the library to develop promotional materials that say the same thing about the library's role in the community. It also reinforces the library's visual identity, thus increasing the probability that potential users will be able to quickly identify materials as coming from the library. By repeating the same message and design over and over, the library can increase the likelihood that potential patrons will hear and absorb their message amid the clutter of all the other messages directed at them daily. People need to get the library's story very quickly. Otherwise it is unlikely that they will spend the time and energy to figure it out.

■ ■ ■ ■

To summarize: Marketing and branding are *not* the same thing. Marketing is a multistep process that consists of both planning and implementation activities. Branding is one of the first steps in a marketing strategy. To develop its brand a library must first articulate a story that explains its role in the community and establishes its uniqueness. It must then find an exciting and attention-grabbing way to tell the story so that potential patrons cannot miss hearing and understanding it. A truly effective marketing process depends on successful branding.

Exercise

Objective

To help clarify the concept of branding for anyone involved in a library-branding project.

Activity

1. Participants should read chapter 1 to develop an understanding of the difference between marketing and branding.

2. Once the staff has read this chapter, ask each person to pick one of the organizations below (all of which are well branded) and spend several days looking at its marketing materials. The marketing can take any form—Internet, television, print, radio, billboards, and so forth.

Dunkin' Donuts	Disney
JetBlue Airways	Mercedes-Benz
McDonald's	Volvo
Starbucks	Salvation Army
Harley-Davidson	Red Cross

3. Once participants have found some marketing materials, ask them to review their materials to see if they can identify the organization's brand story and the basic elements of the brand look. Are the brand story and look consistent, or do they change to match the marketing materials? Develop a central location where the participants can comment on what they found and review what other staff members found. This can be as simple as a bulletin board or notebook in a staff common room, but you may find a virtual collaborative work space to be more effective. If your library does not have a virtual location, such as a staff blog or wiki, where staff can easily write ideas and thoughts to be shared with others, there are several free or low-cost online work spaces available, including PBwiki (http://pbwiki.com), Basecamp (www.basecamphq.com), WebEx (www.webex.com), and activeCollab.com (www.activecollab.com).

4. Ask participants to look at examples of your library's marketing efforts. Can they identify your library's brand story and its look? If not, what is missing? Again ask them to post their results to a central location.

5. Finally, ask participants to start looking carefully at branding they see everyday—it is all around them. Ask them to post notes both when they see something that they think is effective and when they see something that does not work. There are no right or wrong answers here. The idea is to start building participants' awareness about branding and to have them think about good and bad branding.

■2■ Why Brand?

Branding is a term used in many different ways in today's world. Products are branded, services are branded, even people have become their own brands. Think about Martha Stewart. She has become such a strong brand that all you have to do is talk about Martha in the context of homes and decorating and everyone immediately understands to whom you are referring and the connotations. The word *brand* seems to be in constant use. The question then arises as to why branding has become such a highly used tool in general and why it can be useful to a library in particular.

A brand is useful because it is a form of shorthand. A brand tells a story about a product or service in a very short, concise way. It tells potential users what they might expect to get from the product if they decide to use it. A brand is a way of signaling very quickly what potential users can expect to find if they open a package or use a specific service.

Some brands tell this story in terms of their product attributes—the specific details that make a product or service look or act a certain way. Attributes can include colors, shapes, size, speed—characteristics that are very specific and concrete. An example might be seen in a car brand that touts the design or speed of a specific model as the most important factor for a consumer. Another example might be a library that talks about the size of its collection or its new building or the good customer service provided by its librarians.

Other brands tell their story in terms of how they can fulfill a more esoteric need that the user has in his life. This is called emotional branding because the stories tend to appeal more to the emotions and less to the intellect of a potential user. An example might be seen in a car maker that talks about how its brand provides safety or status to the purchaser. A skin care product might imply that its product will make its users feel young and vibrant. A library might tell its patrons that it provides them with a connection to their community. Emotional branding is generally seen as more

? Frequently Asked Question

Is a brand important for every type of library (public, academic, special)?

Branding is important for every type of library. It is particularly useful to public libraries that have to continuously justify their existence in ways that an academic or special library might not have to. However, in an era when so much is available for free on the Internet it makes sense for every library to articulate its reason for being in terms that are absolutely clear to both users and funders.

powerful than attribute branding because emotions themselves are so powerful. If you can develop a brand that taps into the emotional perspective of your potential users, then odds are that you have developed a powerful story about your library in the minds of those individuals.

Given how much information in general, and advertising in particular, the average American encounters in any given day, the ability to convey a substantial amount of information in a short amount of time in an attention-grabbing way can obviously be an important tool when telling a brand story. Both attribute-based and emotion-based branding can be useful ways of telling that story.

Consider the proliferation of cheap and free information in today's society. Libraries used to have the monopoly on providing free information to the public. People did not have access to large book collections or databases of people with similar interests across the country. They had to go to a library to get the information they needed. In contrast, today there are multiple sources to provide information about more subjects than the average person could absorb in a lifetime—libraries, the Internet, books, magazines, radio, television, and so forth.

Here are some simple facts that reinforce this point:

The expansion of the Internet (source: www.domaintools.com)

> 1985—6 domain names registered
>
> 2007—Over 91 million domain names registered

The increase in cell phone usage (source: www.infoplease.com)

> 1994—16 million American subscribers
>
> 2005—194 million American subscribers

The proliferation of blogs (source: www.blogherald.com)

    2002—none

    2007—over 60 million

The proliferation of podcasts (source: Pew Internet and American Life Project)

    2002—none

    2006—over 34 million Americans have listened to a podcast

Because people cannot possibly go through all of these information sources to find what they want, they develop a shortcut for figuring out their best choice. This shortcut is called a consideration set. An individual researches and tries out different products that could possibly fulfill a specific need (like the need for information). Then when that person has the same need in the future, she does not have to go back and research all options again. She has developed a set of products (a consideration set) that she knows will meet her needs and she limits her consideration to these products. This allows her to ignore all of the other hundreds or even thousands of products that *might* meet her needs in the future.

This is how the average consumer limits the amount of information he needs to absorb and carry with him from day to day. A brand is an important tool in this process because it helps a product stand out and be recognized as different from other similar products. It also helps a consumer understand quickly through its brand message what makes it unique. Consumers will not spend a great deal of time building a consideration set, so they need to grasp the nature of a product quickly—a brand helps them do that. Unless a brand is part of a potential user's consideration set, it will not even get a chance to meet that person's needs. Therefore, if libraries want to be part of the information consumer's consideration set, they need to have a brand that can tell their story, and they need to make sure that the story is told regularly.

Libraries are struggling to find a new definition of their value in today's society. Their traditional role as a place to go for books and information is probably not enough to keep them relevant in the information age. Therefore, they keep seeking new directions and ways of serving their communities. Some libraries are becoming community centers. Others are specializing in specific areas, such as genealogy or literacy skills. As libraries start to define and articulate their new roles, they will need to share that information with a public who may well be unfamiliar with the new concepts and may already have consideration sets that fill the role that the library aspires to. A brand will help tell the new story.

For example, a library might decide that it wants to be known as a quiet place where people in its community can relax and connect with each other on a casual basis. However, a Starbucks can be seen as playing the same basic role in a community. If Starbucks is top-of-mind for consumers when they want a quiet place to relax, the public library will not even be part of their thought process. However, if a library has established a strong brand story about its role in the community, a consumer looking for a casual place to relax will be more likely to consider both the library and Starbucks. A brand will help make sure that the library is among the choices when consumers make decisions about what service will best meet their needs.

Finally, a brand is important to a library because it provides an excellent way of focusing an organization's energies in one direction. If everyone in a library understands the library's story and how that story should be told both verbally and visually, then everyone should be moving in the same direction. When all staff members have a clear definition of the library's role in the community, it becomes much easier to evaluate library services and ensure that those services are focused in one consistent direction. A brand story becomes a signpost to an organization, providing direction and specificity about the path forward.

★ Suggestion for Success

Be able to explain why branding is important

Make sure you, the project leader, can articulate why a brand is important for a library. Even if you have a very supportive organization, at some point someone will want to know why on earth branding matters to a library. The project leader will need to be able to state the reasons quickly and clearly.

■ ■ ■ ■

To summarize: A brand is a form of shorthand that allows you to tell a potential library user a story about your library—what makes your library special and why the person should consider using your library. Branding is important to libraries because it enables them to tell their story quickly and efficiently, allows them to communicate what the library sees as its new role in today's society, and helps keep library staff focused in the same direction.

Exercise

Objective

To develop an understanding among your Core Team of the difference between attribute branding and emotional branding.

Activity

Once your Core Team is formed, explain to them the difference between attribute-based and emotion-based branding. Then ask them to find three examples of each. At the second meeting of your Core Team ask members to discuss what they found and why they think their brands fall into one category or the other. Ask them which type of marketing resonates more strongly with them and why. Note: There is no specific conclusion to this activity. Its purpose is to start developing team members' awareness of the different types of branding that exist and what makes them powerful.

▪3▪ Who Should Be Involved in Branding?

Now that we have established the fact that a brand can be a useful and important tool for a library, the next question to ask is who should be involved in the process of developing a library's brand. If your library does not have an existing brand (or if you plan to totally revise the brand you do have), the answer to that question is those individuals who care about the library and are involved in the library's running or who might have a particular interest in the impact or the outcome of the branding process on the library.

Identifying Participants in the Branding Process

Many who care about the branding process are very easy to identify—patrons or staff or faculty members being obvious ones. However, whether you are developing a new brand or revising an existing brand, to make sure that you have identified all possible relevant individuals, you should consider the following questions:

When the library develops a new brand or revises an existing brand, who might be affected and to what degree? For example:

- Patrons might be affected to a high degree because they will start seeing a new or revised brand logo or brand story and it needs to make sense to them.
- Library staff might also be substantially affected because they will need to understand what a new or revised brand strategy means in terms of the everyday work they do.
- The library board or college faculty might be somewhat affected because they might be questioned by the public

Suggestion for Success

Involve the right people

Make sure you get the right people involved in the brand-development process. Think about who could be influential in this process and then find roles that will involve them in what happens. You need both leaders and creative thinkers to develop a good brand and have it work.

as to what the new or revised branding is about and why it was put in place.

- If current board members or faculty were part of a prior branding process, you will need to understand the degree to which they are attached to the old brand so that you can manage any alienation they might feel about changes.

Who might have an interesting perspective about the current or potential role of the library in the community?

- Generally library users are consulted about this question, but nonusers may well have some valuable thoughts.
- Libraries are trying to define a meaningful role not just for today but for the future. Consider talking to not-so-obvious users, such as teenagers, since they will be the library users of the future.

Who might most strongly oppose changing or adjusting the library's current story or the process of developing a story?

- Do not forget older patrons and major donors to the library.
- Consider anyone involved in the prior development of a library brand.

Who knows the library better than anyone?

- Seek opinions from older staff members, older patrons, individuals who have grown up in the community, kids who spend every day after school at the library, and similar groups.

Who does not spend a lot of time at the library but is associated with similar cultural organizations in your town?

- Artists, writers, and musicians are likely to have unique points of view and beneficial skills to contribute to the branding project.

Who needs to be consulted to make sure you are addressing political issues in your community?

- Town managers, other politicians, and community leaders can both add worthwhile information to the branding process and help spread the branding story.

Creating Teams

Once you have developed your preliminary list of participants and discovered (to your horror) that it contains forty or fifty individuals, stop and take a deep breath. You do not need to put all of these people on one committee. Instead, you should think about dividing the group into three teams: the Core Team, the Checkpoint Team, and the Support Team.

The Core Team

The Core Team should be composed of all individuals who absolutely must be involved in the process from beginning to end. If these people do not participate actively in the branding process, then it is guaranteed to fail. At least one informal leader from the library's staff (that is, a person who can drive opinion simply by voicing her perspective) should be included, as should key trustees or members of your board. If people on your staff have an understanding of design or branding or marketing, they should be included because they will be very helpful. The library director or assistant director or both should also be involved because they are crucial decision makers. I would suggest limiting your Core Team to six to ten people.

Tip

As you consider who should be involved in your branding process, be sure to include individuals at both ends of the age spectrum. Younger people can provide a great deal of relevant input. They will tell you if your branding ideas make sense to their generation. People age sixty-five and older are also important to include. Seniors are frequently among the most regular and loyal patrons of libraries. Not to consider their input would be to ignore key members of your library community.

Suggestion for Success

Embrace your role as project leader

As project leader you need to be a combination of facilitator and leader. You need to lead when a group gets bogged down, you need to have a vision of what branding can bring to your library, and you need to be willing to make the decisions about your brand. However, at the same time you need to be able to recognize a good idea when you see it, regardless of the source, and you need to be willing to change your approach if a better way of doing the branding work is identified by a team member.

The Checkpoint Team

The Checkpoint Team should be brought into the branding process at vital junctures. The involvement of these people is important, but the process will not succeed or fail based on their inclusion. Generally, I believe that most members of a library's board fall into this category, as do library staff. They need to understand and buy in to the process. However, this can be accomplished by a consistent and thorough communication process via e-mail and telephone rather than by including everyone on the Core Team. Longtime library users also tend to fall into this category. They are often very passionate about the library and believe very strongly in its role in the community. They want to feel part of the process and will usually support what is happening at the library as long as they are in the know. Another important group to consider is major donors to the library. Many institutional participants (such as donors) feel very strongly about all aspects of the organizations they support. Rather than alienate these individuals, you want to harness their positive energy. The Checkpoint Team may range in size from as few as twenty individuals to as many as fifty. Usually e-mail and telephone are the most effective tools for communication with them. The decision about whether to hold meetings with the Checkpoint Team will depend on the team's membership. I think that actual meetings are unnecessary in most cases as long as you keep team members informed about the project's progress. Nonetheless, you may decide it is important to hold one or two actual meetings with this group to share information and gather input.

Suggestion for Success

Get the library director on board

Make sure the library director understands and supports the concept of brand development. The director is always important, whether or not he is directly involved in the project, because he is the final arbiter of what will and will not happen in your library. You can develop the best brand in the world, but if the director does not like it or does not want to use it, that brand will most likely never see the light of day.

The Support Team

The Support Team is made up of individuals who need general information about the progress of the branding process but probably only at the beginning, middle, and end of the work. This might include the general public, the town newspaper, local political leaders, and the majority of library users. These people are not going to create problems or hurdles for the library during the branding process. However, if they understand why the library is doing branding, they can potentially help by lending positive support.

Team Roles

Once you have organized your list of participants into teams, you should find that your enterprise becomes a little simpler in focus. Your Core Team should be six to ten people. This is the primary group that will support you in the branding process. The role of this group is twofold. First, they should provide you with advice, counsel, input, and perspective. They are your source for a broad-based view of the branding work. Second, this group should help you with the actual work of creating the brand. For example, if you are planning to do a press release about the branding work, it helps to have someone on the Core Team who is familiar with press releases and can write at least a basic one for you. There are many steps to the branding process, and if you are the only person charged with creating the brand, then assistance will be critical to your success. You will be communicating with the Core Team in person, on the telephone, and via e-mail and newsletters. You should plan to use all tools at your disposal to keep this group involved and participating in the branding process.

The role of the Checkpoint Team (which with anywhere from twenty to fifty individuals will probably be substantially larger than the Core Team) is to provide input and feedback about the more general issues the project faces. For example, you may want to determine if there is a great deal of ownership in your community for an existing brand logo. To do this, you might field a short survey to your Checkpoint Team to ask for input. If there is strong loyalty to the existing logo, then members of the Checkpoint Team can provide input and direction about how to proceed with making changes. A Checkpoint Team frequently has well-connected individuals on it. They may not be key decision makers themselves, but they are often in touch with such decision makers and can help make sure you have touched base with all key constituents before moving ahead with significant decisions. Telephone and e-mail updates are typically the best ways of communicating with your Checkpoint Team.

The Support Team does not really have a specific role in the branding process. They are involved at a very general level, primarily to make sure that they feel included and that they will not cause unexpected problems during the branding process. Some libraries do not even see a need for a Support Team; others find it useful. You can usually stay in touch with this group via general newsletters, e-mails, and articles in your local newspaper. If you live in a highly politicized community (meaning one in which any civic issue brings out a lot of strong opinions on both sides), it makes sense to think carefully about how to communicate with this group to ensure that they are aware of your branding activities and, you can hope, support them.

Working with Your Core Team

Once your key participants have been identified and categorized, the next issue is to determine how to get your Core Team involved in the branding process. Sometimes it is as simple as asking an individual to participate and he agrees. However, frequently there is more work involved. The following is a simple approach to consider using:

1. Develop a short (no more than one page), to-the-point case statement. Many libraries are familiar with the case statements used to support fund-raising efforts—this statement is similar, only the focus is different. The case statement should justify the branding project by providing the following information: (a) a summary of the specific activities that make up the branding project, (b) a definition of the objective of the branding process, (c) what is entailed if an individual becomes involved in the project (attend three meetings lasting two hours each, read four documents, etc.—make sure you are as specific and detailed as possible), and (d) why the project is important for the library. The case statement should not be longer than one

page. Bullet points are preferred and the language should be very simple—you must assume that the reader has absolutely no background in this issue at all (although many of the participants probably will). The case statement should not be longer than one page. (No, repeating this three times is not a mistake—I am trying to make a point!) Give the case statement to several individuals outside the library (friends, family) and ask them to read it and comment on its clarity and the degree to which it gives the information they would need if they were to join the team.

2. Write an e-mail (or a letter, depending on what seems appropriate for your community) to each possible participant and attach a copy of the case statement. Indicate that you will call in a few days to answer any additional questions and to find out how the individual is feeling about the invitation—and then make sure you follow up as promised. Some invitees may respond immediately and tell you that they will participate. Others may wait and join only if you have a direct conversation with them.

3. When people accept your invitation, immediately phone to thank them for getting involved. Remind each person of the first group meeting and send out a packet of information. The packet of information should have the case statement (again), samples of any branding that the library currently employs, and some questions for the individual to consider when looking at the branding materials (see the exercise at the end of this chapter). Your goal is to give new team members some work to think about and start to review immediately. This should encourage them to get invested and involved in the project.

The bottom line is to remember that although most of the participants in the project will be highly committed, like all people in today's society, they are probably very busy and stressed by the obligations of their day-to-day life. You thus need to keep all information you give them short and to the point. For example, write using bullet points and short paragraphs, and tell them only what they need to know. If you approach things this way, you are more likely to attract individuals who will provide valuable input. A very effective way of sharing information with a short-term but intensely focused work group like this is to set up a shared workspace online. In the workspace you can have a blog for ongoing comments and thoughts about the project, post minutes from meetings, and place copies of work as it is developed. This tends to be much more efficient than e-mailing, and it helps to build a sense of connection between team members.

If you are only planning to update your brand, you do not have to go through the whole process of identifying Core, Checkpoint, and Support teams. You do still need to identify those individuals who will have the greatest interest in the project. However, there may not be as many and you may be able to do much of the work using the accumulated knowledge and background of your staff. When I first went through this process in Wakefield, my director and I were updating an existing brand, not developing a new brand from scratch. We decided to focus our energies on involving the staff, most of whom had worked at the library for anywhere from five to thirty years. Our thoughts were that they were as vested and knowledgeable as anyone else we might find, and their energy and input would provide us with the correct direction. In essence, the staff became our Core Team. We then used the library's board and Friends of the Library as our Checkpoint Team. This method seemed to work very efficiently and could be a perfectly viable option for many libraries, depending on their circumstances. If your library is part of a county system, you will probably need to develop only a Core Team, which might consist totally of library staff. You will have to decide what works best for your library type and system.

■ ■ ■ ■

To summarize: To develop a brand, a library will need to organize up to three teams: the Core Team—six to ten of the most involved individuals; the Checkpoint Team—twenty to fifty people that will provide additional input and help, and the Support Team—all individuals that need to be kept aware of the process. Once potential team members have been identified, they must be recruited. To aid in the recruiting process the project manager should develop a short case statement that articulates what the project is about and what will be expected of volunteers.

 Suggestions for Success

Be open to input, but be willing to lead

Branding is a creative enterprise. Everyone will want to share their thoughts, which I generally try to be open to because good ideas can come from anywhere and everywhere. However, given that branding is a very subjective process it is almost impossible to implement it by consensus. Someone will need to make the decisions, and that should be the person with the most passion and involvement—the project leader.

Exercise

Objective

To initiate the Core Team's evaluation of the library's existing branding materials.

Activity

Prepare a handout for each new Core Team member prior to the first meeting of the team. It should be attached to examples of the library's current branding materials and include the following questions:

- Would you know that all of these materials come from the same organization? What visual cues tell you that they are from the same place, or what cues are missing that would indicate that they are related?
- Based on these materials, what story do you think the library is telling about itself?
- Do you like these materials? If yes, why? If no, why not?
- Do you think these materials convey an attribute-based or emotion-based message? Do you think it is a message that will resonate in the community?

At the first meeting of the Core Team discuss each person's response to these questions. If there is little or no consistency in branding materials, the Core Team will start to discover that for themselves, which will help vest them in the branding process.

■4■ The Ideal Brand

Before starting work on your own library brand, you may find it helpful to consider what a great brand looks like. A great brand is a product or service that you remember clearly and is part of your ongoing thought process or consideration set. You remember easily what the brand's message is, you understand how you would use the brand's product or service, and you understand how the brand will be meaningful to your life.

The Key Elements of a Great Brand

There are four key elements that help ensure a brand is great—a clear, meaningful, unique message; an attention-grabbing visual identity; consistent use; and an ongoing effort to ensure the brand stays honest.

A Clear, Meaningful, Unique Message

A great brand has a succinct and utterly clear message. There is no doubt about what a good brand says about itself and no doubt about how that brand wants to be viewed by potential users. Its message is straightforward and unambiguous. Any piece of marketing material will tell the same story as any other piece. A good example of this is Apple Computer. Apple has always presented itself as the computer for people who "think different." Apple has never tried to appeal to the whole world and in fact has made a place for itself in an incredibly competitive marketplace by sticking to its role as a product for a very specific audience. The company supports this message in every aspect of its branding. Its packaging is unique, its products are unique, and it sells its products in its own special stores. The company does everything it can to promote the concept of Apple products being suitable for those who think differently.

A great brand has a message that is meaningful to its audience. You can deliver a clear, exciting message, but if it has no relevance to the audience, then it will have no impact. You need to make sure that your audience understands your message not only because it is clear but also because they care about the message. For example, VWs are targeted to a young, hip audience. Members of this audience probably do not care as much about a car's safety record as they do about its being cool and suited to their lifestyle. Therefore, a message about safety just will not be particularly meaningful or relevant. This is why it is important to understand your target audience. If you are not familiar with their specific characteristics, you will not be able to figure out what kind of message will be meaningful or relevant to them.

Some brands may have a very clearly defined target audience and a message that suits that audience, but they take a wrong turn and change their message. Talbots, a company specializing in women's clothing, is a good example. The company always sold high-quality, classically styled clothes and accessories to women over age thirty. In the 1990s the company decided to try to bring in a new, younger consumer and redesigned their clothes to be more youthful and trendy. The strategy worked, and younger consumers did buy their clothes. However, Talbots forgot to think about the message this change was sending to its existing consumers—older women. That group did not like the new styles, felt the stores were no longer appropriate to their age group, and abandoned the company in droves. The new brand message had no relevance to the lives of more mature women, and, unfortunately for Talbots, they were much bigger spenders than their younger counterparts. Talbots eventually realized its error and started shifting its approach again. The company went back to a more traditional brand message and brought back its original consumer base while retaining younger women who liked a more classic style of clothing. The revised brand message seems to have worked because the company figured out who their target audience truly was and what was relevant to that group.

A great brand tells potential users what makes its product unique or special. You do not want to make the same claim as every other brand that your potential patron is thinking about using. You want to tell your target audience that your brand has something distinctive and wonderful that they cannot get anywhere else—something that makes you different. If you decide to focus your message on a specific component of your service, consider whether that service can be duplicated somewhere else. Yes, the public library offers great customer service, but so do book stores. Yes, the library offers free information, but so does the Internet. You do not want to select a "difference" that is in truth widely found and easily available. Otherwise it becomes much more difficult to stand out from all of the other brands claiming the same thing as your brand.

If you decide that you need to stick with the same message as other brands, you can still find a way to make your brand special. Think about your library and what it offers. You might do something the best. You might be the first to do something. You might have special skills that make your delivery better than anyone else's. Find a way to own your message and make it unique to your brand.

Beer companies are among the least successful creators of brands. They all talk about the same qualities (taste, ingredients) and provide very little information that allows a consumer to distinguish one from another. The result is that although beer companies run wonderful, funny, creative ads that people talk about over and over, consumers rarely remember which company ran which ad. All the fun and creativity essentially are wasted.

Ultimately, your brand's message has to be remembered quickly and easily. Do not forget that the message is meant to implant the image of your brand in the mind (or consideration set) of potential users. If they cannot remember your brand message, they certainly will not make your brand part of their consideration set. An attention-grabbing visual identity is one element that can help ensure speedy recall of your brand message.

An Attention-Grabbing Visual Identity

A great brand has a visual identity (logo) that supports the brand story in powerful, attention-getting, visual terms. You do not want a logo that recedes into the background or is hard to understand or needs to be explained. A great brand has a logo that is interesting to look at and that uses colors and typefaces to support the brand message. So, if you are telling a story about how progressive and forward thinking your brand is, you probably should not use a medieval typeface and sepia tones in your logo.

A great example of a successful logo is the swoosh used by Nike. The swoosh suggests speed and movement and energy—all factors that Nike wants to promote as part of its brand. In fact, the swoosh has become so widely recognizable that Nike can use it alone in advertising; no further identification is necessary.

Many brands have visually interesting logos that catch your attention and stick in your memory. For instance, the Coca-Cola logo has become so commonly recognized that even when different words are written in the logo's font, people read them as Coca-Cola. That shows the power of an arresting visual image.

Libraries frequently have problems with their visual identity because they have to work with a logo that has been developed by someone who lacks professional design expertise. The results can be amateurish, outdated, and lacking in relevance to the library of today. However, if the logo has been used for a long enough period of time, it might evoke instant recognition and a great deal of faithful care and concern. Try to understand how your various library constituents feel about your existing logo before you decide to develop a completely new one. There might be powerful and useful equity in the old logo that you can transfer to a revised design.

Consistent Use

A good brand repeats its message over and over and over. See if you know what brands the following messages represent:

> Good to the last drop
>
> It's time to make the donuts
>
> The best part of waking up is . . . in your cup

The answers are Maxwell House Coffee, Dunkin' Donuts, and Folgers Coffee. What made these brands so easily recognizable? The consistent (and constant) repetition of the brand message over long periods of time—in Maxwell House's case, for over a hundred years. Interestingly enough, if an organization uses the same brand message long enough, consumers will actually resist changing it because they are so vested in it. This happened at Maxwell House. In the 1990s the company tried to change its "Good to the Last Drop" brand message. They spent hundreds of thousands of dollars developing and promoting a new message and then found that the only thing people ever recalled was "Good to the Last Drop." Finally, the company gave up and went back to the original. Why fight success? Bottom line, no matter what your message, if you say it the same way over and over, people will start to recognize and remember it. If you change messages every year or six months, no one will have time to remember your brand message, much less include it in their consideration set.

Consistency also means that you use your brand message and visuals in the same way on all of your marketing materials. You will need to define how the brand should be used and then ask your library to stick within those parameters. How to develop such brand standards will be discussed in chapter 8.

Ongoing Effort to Keep the Brand Honest

A strong brand is one that is honest: it delivers what it says it will deliver. It does not promise too much (use this toothpaste and you will be rich and sexy) and it lives up to what it does promise. An example of this is the Volvo brand, which promises safety. Volvos are indeed among the safest cars on the road, and the company has the statistics to prove it.

When you develop your library's message, make sure that you do not claim something that you cannot deliver. Do not say that your library is the friendliest place in town if your staff does not support that notion and act accordingly. Do not say you are the center of the community if in fact you have very few community resources and do not really promote your town. If you use a misleading message to attract people into your library, they will be disappointed. Disappointed users not only do not come back but also have a habit of telling many of their friends about their disappointment, which is never good for the library.

How to Put a Great Brand to Work

Once you develop a great brand, you need to put it to work. The simple rule of thumb is that you should use your brand everywhere you can. Your brand should be on any communication that goes out from your library to your community. This means that your brand should be on your business cards, stationery, envelopes, labels, signage, website, and any promotional pieces that you develop, such as posters, postcards, and news releases. When you write an article for the newspaper, ask the editor to publish it with your library's logo. If you do PowerPoint presentations in front of faculty or the Chamber of Commerce, your slides should have the library's logo on them. If you have name tags for staff members, they should display the library's logo. You want your brand to be ubiquitous. The more frequently people see your brand, the more likely they are to connect it to the library, to remember your brand message, and to include the library in their consideration set.

■ ■ ■ ■

To summarize: A brand is great if it has a clear, meaningful, unique message and an attention-grabbing visual identity; is used consistently; and is honest.

Exercise

Objective

To help your Core Team develop an understanding of what makes a brand great.

Activity

Ask your Core Team members to keep a very brief, one-day diary in which they record all brands that they run into. Ask them to score each brand on a scale of 1 to 5 (1 = fails to do, 5 = does extremely well).

1. Has a clear meaningful, unique message that can be remembered
2. Has an attention-grabbing visual identity
3. Is used consistently
4. Is honest

At a meeting of your Core Team, review and discuss what they discovered. Do they agree that the highest scoring brands are great? If not, why not? At this meeting, do the same exercise with whatever brand your library currently has. Do the team members' scores tend to agree, or are they quite divergent? Does the library brand score high or low on the scale? Where is there a need for improvement? Have the team discuss general issues that they see. This will provide good preparation for your library's brand audit, a process that is delineated in chapter 5.

■5■   The Brand Audit

Before you jump into the branding process, it makes sense to understand where your library is today with respect to branding. This is the best place to start whether your library has a well-established brand that has been used for years or the extent of your library's brand is just its name. In either case understanding how your library has been telling its story will help you identify what you need to do to move forward and either develop a new brand or revamp your existing brand. That understanding can be most readily gained by performing a brand audit. Such an audit is a review of your brand as it stands today so that you can identify where it fits on a continuum of development. That information will allow you to determine your next steps forward.

A full brand audit is meant to review where your brand stands with respect to the four factors that make a brand great: message, visual identity, consistency of delivery, and honesty (see chapter 4). A brand audit is carried out in four steps. Each step is meant to gather input about your brand from important users of your library. You may determine that you do not need to do all four steps because you have already gotten feedback from some of the brand users. That is fine. Your object is to understand the current status of your brand. If you already have information that helps you do that, you can adapt the content of this chapter to meet your specific needs.

The first step will be to have your Core Team audit your brand. Given that they are the key members of the branding team, it is obviously critical to get their input. Your second step will be to get feedback from your staff and board about your brand. The third step will be to get input from your patrons about your brand. Fourth, you will examine all this input and use it to determine the status of your brand today with respect to its message, its visual identity, its consistency, and its honesty.

Step One: Obtaining the Core Team's Perspective

Go through the exercise at the end of this chapter. It will help you collect your materials for your brand audit. Essentially you are putting all of your branding materials as they exist today in one place so that they can be reviewed as a summary representation of your brand.

Invite your Core Team to a meeting, but do not define the specifics. Let everyone into the meeting room at the same time and give them two minutes to look at the materials that you have posted. Then ask the team members to write down answers to the following questions:

1. When you look at all of the materials, is it clear that they all come from the same organization (yes or no)?

2. What organization originated these materials?

3. Is there a consistent look to the materials—in other words, does one piece look like it comes from the same place as another piece (yes or no)? If you said yes, what is done consistently? What is not done consistently?

4. Based on looking at these materials, what do you think this organization's message is? Do you like its message? Do you like the library's look? If not, why not?

5. If there is a clear message, do you think the library delivers on that message? For example, if the library says it is the heart of the community, do you think that is true? Why or why not?

Once your team has answered these questions in writing, ask the members to share their answers with the group while you take notes on a flip chart. Your goal is to determine if there is consensus around the answers to the questions and to develop a profile of how your team regards the library's current brand. There are several potential results to this evaluation:

1. Everyone agrees on what the materials say and look like. If they think there is a consistent message and a consistent look to the materials, then it indicates that they feel the brand is in reasonable shape and that only some minor work may need to be done to continue using the brand as is.

2. No one agrees on the answers and there is no shared perspective. This may be because there aren't enough materials to develop a shared perspective or it may be because those materials are just not consistent. In this case, your brand needs substantial work because it is not conveying a consistent message to its audience.

> **① Tip**
>
> When evaluating the library's current brand, start by asking all team members to keep in mind that the objective of this exercise (and any future exercises) is to identify opportunities for continuous improvement, not to make judgments about bad or good. Such an approach will avoid alienating anyone on your Core Team who might have worked on developing the existing brand and will keep the focus on improvement and excellence rather than faultfinding—something that is never a productive use of time.

3. People understand the library's message or look or both, but for whatever reason they do not like them or think they are not right for the library. This requires rethinking the brand message.

Summarize the feedback. Make sure you understand the team's responses with respect to the brand's message and visual imagery, such as its logo or colors. These are the two key areas in which you are trying to understand what work needs to be done. Then move on to step 2.

Step Two: Obtaining the Perspectives of the Staff and Board

Step 2 in an audit is to get input about your brand from your staff and your board. I recommend talking to both groups because you may get very different perspectives from each. Given that staff in particular often have very strong points of view about the library's brand, it is important to give them an opportunity to articulate those. I would suggest that you go through the same process with the staff and the board that you went through with your Core Team. This is best accomplished by working with each group separately. Give each group a brief exposure to your collected branding materials. Then ask them to write answers to the questions in step 1. Once they have done this, encourage the group to discuss their responses while you evaluate the extent of their agreement. Is there consensus either for or against the branding materials, or is there a mixed result?

Once you have completed this process with your board and staff, summarize your results in writing. Again, try to make sure that you understand the responses specifically with respect to the brand's message and visual imagery. Compare the results to what you got from your Core Team. Can you see any consistency in how people feel about the branding materials?

Step Three: Obtaining the Public's Perspective

The third group to consider is your public. Generally the public's input can be very insightful and helpful. However, because they are an external audience rather than an internal one, you will need to take a somewhat different approach than you took with the first two groups. You can usually collect most of the information from this group through a paper or online survey. You will be looking for information related to the following key questions:

1. Is the public hearing your brand message (if you have one) and are they hearing that message consistently? To get the answer to this you can ask patrons an open-ended question such as "What do you think is the role of the library in the community?" Or you can provide them with choices and see which ones they choose (ask them to indicate all that apply): the library is a community center, the library is the intellectual center of the community, the library is the center of civic pride in the community, and so forth.

2. Does your public think that the library's message is appropriate, and do they have any ideas about how to change or clarify that message? Once you have asked about the library's message, you can present a number of sample messages and ask respondents to pick the one choice that they think is *best* for their library. Or you can ask them to tell you what role they think the library *should* take in the community.

3. Is your public aware of any visual imagery (logo, colors, typeface) that relates to your brand? You can elicit such information by asking your patrons to tell you what the library logo looks like—what images and colors are used. If you make this an open-ended question, then you will really discover the degree to which people are aware of the logo. Because you are not providing them with choices, they have to come up with the imagery from memory.

Tip

Do not be afraid to look at what other libraries have done and borrow questions from them. Librarians tend to be very collegial in nature, so if you e-mail a few to ask their thoughts about their survey, they will generally be more than happy to help you out with input about the success or failure of various questions. No one minds copying. In fact the majority seem to see it as a form of flattery because it means they came up with a good idea.

Your patrons are probably the best situated to tell you if your branding materials as they exist today are working. Because they are the audience for your message, their reactions can tell you to what degree they are getting that message. Although your questions may be short and simple, the responses are likely to provide rich information about the effectiveness of your message and visual imagery.

The simplest way of getting input from your patrons is via a survey. Today many library patrons are comfortable with computers. That allows you to put a survey on your website and ask patrons for feedback. Or you can use an online survey instrument like SurveyMonkey.com. I would augment any online survey by putting a paper version at the circulation desk. Often even computer-comfortable patrons prefer to answer a survey on paper—they feel that paper somehow makes their feedback more direct.

Once your library users have completed the survey, you will need to review the information and determine if there is any consistency in their responses about the brand message and the brand look.

Step Four: Compiling and Interpreting All Findings

You will then be ready to put together the feedback from all three audits to determine your next steps. Start by looking at the degree of consistency in the responses. If the feedback about both your library's message and its visual imagery is very similar across all three groups, your library has probably been putting out a consistent branding message. In this situation you need to decide if that is the message you want to continue using, and if it is, you can for the most part continue on course.

If the feedback from your audits varies widely, then you will need to sort out what it means. Is the lack of consistency related to the brand's message, its visual imagery, or both? Or is the message perceived as clear but lacking in honesty? If you can isolate whether the respondents' differing perceptions stem from the message or the visuals, you will know where you need to start in the branding process.

Be prepared to find out that library users remember your logo but do not know your message. Often libraries do a great job with their visual imagery (the brand logo) because it is the part of the branding process that everyone understands. However, many libraries do not have a clear message, and this is most often where lack of consistency is discovered. Variations may occur because your message has never been clearly defined or because different parts of your organization communicate different messages. Or it may just be that your audience does not like the message you are using.

If you think your message is the issue but you are not sure what the specific problem is, answer the following questions:

1. Does your audience know what your message is? If so, you are probably being reasonably consistent in putting out that message.

2. Did your audit indicate that people responded positively to your message? If they remembered your message and responded well to it, then you are in good shape. However, if they remembered the message but did not like it, then you need to rethink your message and focus on developing one that resonates better with your audience. A negative response might also indicate that the message is not honest, meaning that the library is promising something in its message but not delivering on it. For example, if a library builds its message around the concept of great customer service but in fact provides poor service, patrons will quickly spot the contradiction. To understand if this is the problem, consider your message carefully and objectively. In some cases the message may be fine, but the library needs to focus on delivering what the message promises.

3. If there was a lack of consistency in the responses (some people knew what the message was and some did not, some people responded well to the message and some did not), go back to the room where you posted all the branding materials and take another look at them, this time on a department-by-department basis. Are the different departments (youth services, reference services, programming) putting out different messages, or do their materials look very different? If so, then your focus should be on delivering the brand consistently, not on the brand itself.

4. To determine if the visual image of your brand is the problem, check the responses from your audit to see whether people remembered what your logo looks like. If you use your logo consistently but people cannot recall it, you need to investigate why the logo fails to make a lasting impression and remedy the situation.

■ ■ ■ ■

To summarize: If you have an existing brand, you will need to start the branding process by evaluating how well your brand operates today. You can accomplish this by doing a brand audit, or review, of all of your current branding materials. During the audit you will review your branding materials with three groups: your Core Team, your board and staff, and your library users. The input from these groups should help you determine how effective your brand is and where any weaknesses lie.

Exercise

Objective

To ensure that you have collected the right materials to perform a brand audit.

Activity

Before you begin you will need to collect all of the branding materials that your library has been using. Consider all of the following materials:

- Letterhead, envelopes, business cards
- Flyers or posters used by the library to promote special events
- Press releases, newspaper articles
- Copies of the library's website, blogs, e-mail newsletters, RSS feeds
- Logos used by the library and the Friends of the Library
- Any materials that the library sells or gives away, such as T-shirts, umbrellas, aprons, and pens
- Be sure to include materials for the library's youth room as well as materials targeted to adults

If your current brand consists of your library's name only, you should still go through this process. Collect examples of any and all communication materials (letterhead, envelopes, business cards, flyers, program announcements) that have your library's name on them. Post and consider them in exactly the same way described for an already established brand.

Once these materials are collected they should be posted all in one place—preferably in a room at your library or, if necessary, in a virtual room online. You do not need to worry about how artfully the materials are displayed. Just put them up on a wall or board so that they can easily be reviewed.

■6■ The Story
Defining Your Message

Whether you are new to the library-branding process or an old hand revising an existing brand, your brand audit should have given you a stronger sense of where your brand stands with respect to the message you are trying to convey. Specifically, your brand audit should have helped you answer the following questions:

1. Does your brand have a clear, consistent, unique message that is meaningful to your audience? This is possible even if the only component of your brand is your library's name.
2. Does your brand have attention-grabbing visual imagery that supports your brand message?
3. Is the brand used consistently?
4. Is the brand message honest?

Your understanding of where your brand stands in terms of each of these questions will direct you toward the work that needs to be done to develop your brand and make it great.

The discussion in this chapter assumes that you have discovered that your message, your visual imagery, your consistency, and your brand honesty are all missing or need work and that you must start at the beginning of the branding process. If you have received positive feedback on one or more elements of your brand as it exists today, you may prefer to read only the sections of this chapter that are most relevant to your specific situation.

The Foundation for All Branding: Your Message

As discussed previously, developing a clear, concise vision of what role your library can take in your patrons' lives is the first and most important thing you can do if you want to market effectively. The starting point for all branding work is your message. Whether you are developing a new brand or revamping an existing brand, you should start with the message. This is the step most frequently overlooked in branding. Libraries think that if they have a logo, they have done their branding. Sometimes this is true if the brand's message is contained in the logo. However, more often than not a logo is just one step in the branding process. One sure way to tell if your library has been delivering a brand message is to ask staff to tell you what the library sees as its role in the community. If they cannot answer or you get many different answers, then you know the organization has not focused on a consistent brand message.

Evaluating Your Message

To determine if you are communicating the right message, you have to start by deciding if your library is what you want it to continue to be. During your brand audit you received feedback from your Core Team, your staff, your board, and your public about how they perceive the library's role today (see chapter 5). Is that what you want to be? Or do you want to start to develop a new vision of the library's role in the community? Here are some questions to consider as you evaluate your current message:

- Is your current message clear? Do potential library users understand what you are saying the library can do for them?
- Are people hearing an accurate message, or is the desired message somehow getting garbled in the translation?
- Is there any lack of consistency in the message being conveyed?
- Is the existing message relevant and meaningful to library's constituents? Is it powerful enough to move the library forward into the future?

My recommendation would be that if there are any issues identified by the above questions or lack of consistency in the feedback that you received, you probably need to rethink and revise your message (or start all over). If you do not have a message about your library defined at all, then all of the feedback you have received to date will provide you with valuable directions for what that message should be.

Matching Your Message to Your Community

To revise or develop your library's story or message, you need a clear understanding of the community in which your library is situated, whether that community is a town or city or college or high school. What is the vision of that community? Where does the community see itself over the next five years? Based on that, you can consider how the library might participate in its community's vision.

For example, my current library is in Brunswick, Maine. Over the next four years Brunswick will be going through a major transformation as its Naval Air Station is closed. This will result in extensive population, employment, and housing changes in Brunswick and its surrounding communities. Therefore, Brunswick is redefining itself, trying to develop a new, productive vision for the future. As my library develops its message or story, it can enhance its usefulness and relevance by defining that message within the context of the Brunswick community vision. If a library tries to develop a message that has no relationship to the community within which it is situated, then it runs the very real risk of becoming irrelevant—particularly in communities going through significant changes. So, given that Brunswick is losing population and jobs and a sizable community base, the library might decide to define itself as a community center—a place where people can come to reconnect and get information about changes taking place in the community. This role has relevance to Brunswick's citizens and makes the public library an integral part of the community's change.

There are several places you can go for information about your community's vision. If your community is a college or university, there is most likely a strategic plan that defines the school's vision for the future. If you work in a public library, you can go to your town or city offices to see if there is a comprehensive plan (which is essentially a strategic plan) that provides the basic information you need. If your town does not have a comprehensive plan, have a discussion with the town manager or other official who runs the community. If that person cannot suggest another document, you could ask for her input instead. If it ends up that you need to do interviews to get the information, make sure you talk to several key town leaders to get a range of viewpoints. If all other options fail, then have your Core Team collect and review whatever information they can and identify their own vision for your community. Sometimes library groups resist expressing a community vision because they feel that it is not their role. In fact, if no one else has identified a community vision, there is no reason why a library team would not be as qualified as any other group. Develop your own community vision and then build the library vision accordingly. At least you will have made an effort to connect your library with your community.

Developing a Message Based on Your Library's Mission or Vision

If your library has a strategic plan, you probably already have the information needed to understand your library's role in its community. If the plan

THE STORY ■ 41

talks about the library's role today, it is called the library's mission. If it talks about the library's desired role in the future, it is probably called the library's vision. Neither the mission nor the vision can be used as a brand message because both are internal, strategic statements meant to guide the direction of a single organization. They are not meant to be articulations of purpose for your public. However, clearly they should be reference points as you define your brand message.

To convert a mission or vision statement into a branding message, you and your Core Team need to determine how that statement can be fine-tuned so that anyone entering the library would understand it immediately. Give team members a copy of the library's vision or mission statement and a copy of the list in appendix B, if you think those terms might be helpful. Then ask each team member to rewrite the statement in simple, easy-to-understand words, using the following format:

_____ provides (or will provide) its users with _____.
[Name of my library]   [need the library meets or will meet]

Being concise and to the point is important. If you have a well-thought-out mission/vision, this exercise should be easy. Have team members read their statements aloud while you write them on a flip chart for the whole team to see. Evaluate what has been written down. The team should challenge itself: Is the thing being provided unique and meaningful to your library users? Could some key words be replaced by more powerful language? Have the team go through appendix B or a thesaurus to find alternatives for their initial language. Then ask them to reevaluate their statements to see if any of the new words work more effectively without sacrificing simplicity and understandability.

Pick out the five statements that seem to resonate most strongly with the team. Then request that they take those choices home, read them to family and friends, and ask those individuals to recall what they heard. Did the listeners get each message right? If not, what language led them astray? Meet as a team again to evaluate the feedback and revise the five choices as necessary. Then, to do some quick additional research, place a survey at your circulation desk or on your website. Present the five revised messages to your library users and ask them to evaluate each one by responding to the following statements:

- I understand this message—there are no words or phrases that confuse me. (True/False/Somewhat)
- I agree with this statement—I think this is or could be the library's role in the community. (True/False/Somewhat)

- I like this message—it has relevance to me and to my life. (True/False/ Somewhat)

Consider the input you receive. It is important that the majority of respondents understand the message, think that it is appropriate for the library, and find it meaningful to their lives. If at least 50 percent of the people surveyed do not answer true to each question about a message, that message should be eliminated from consideration. If none of the messages receive good scores, it may be that your library's mission/vision statement needs to be revised before a brand message can be built from it. Assuming that at least two of your messages do ring true with your users, pick one to use as the branding message. It will then become the focal point of your marketing messages.

How to Develop a Brand Message without a Mission or Vision

If your library does not have a mission or vision, you can still define the basic information such a statement would contain to use as a framework for your branding activities. At the beginning of this chapter you learned how to get information about your community's vision for the future. Working with your Core Team, you can build on that information to move forward and develop a branding message.

Start the process by asking your Core Team to consider the information collected about your community's vision. Then ask them to articulate what role the library plays in today's community and what role they think it should play in tomorrow's community. At this point you do not have to worry about crafting a carefully defined statement. Rather, you want ideas to flow freely so that you can arrive at a general framework for moving forward. As the group works on this task, encourage them not to get too specific. Instead, help them to identify broad concepts, such as your library should be a com-

Tip

When you do your patron survey, do not allow it to be any longer than four or five questions, and keep the timeline for collecting information from your patrons short—two weeks is probably more than enough, especially if you are doing the survey online. People have a tendency either to fill out a survey as soon as they see it or to put it away and forget about it. A longer timetable just draws out the collection period, it rarely pulls in more information.

munity center or your library should be the intellectual center of your community or your library is the civic center of your community. Keep in mind that your statement should be simple and free of jargon. Everyone in the library needs to understand it without a long explanation.

Do an initial edit of the ideas. You should be able to compile a list of five options that seem reasonable. Use the format identified in the previous section: "[Name of my library] provides (or will provide) its users with [need the library meets or will meet]." Do not be afraid to put ideas out there that seem a little crazy or far-fetched. Part of your role in this process is both to read the current perspective of your community and to act as a leader in identifying viable roles for your library that may never occur to your community members.

Once you come up with five sentences that define potential roles for your library, test them. Follow the procedure recommended earlier in this chapter for libraries that already have a mission or vision: use a survey to gather your patrons' thoughts and, based on their input, identify which role seems to resonate with the most people. This role then becomes the focus of your brand message.

A note of caution: A choice my library once gave patrons in a survey described the library as a provider of free resources. This turned out to be somewhat problematic because any good, red-blooded American always chooses the option with the word *free* in it. That is something I learned as a marketer and then forgot. If you throw *free* into the equation, it is always the top choice, even if, in fact, it might not be the best choice. I would not want to describe my public library as a source of free resources for three reasons. First, because it is not true, as any taxpayer will tell you. Second, because *free* can be easily copied by other organizations, if they so choose. And third, *free* is an attribute of what a library offers—it is not a descriptor of the role a library can play in a community. Try to avoid this mistake!

Attributes or Emotion or Both?

Make no mistake: defining your library's message or story is not easy. Librarians will want to talk about their wonderful customer service or their large collections or their special archives or their programming. These are all the things that libraries do wonderfully well and that help make them special institutions. Indeed, some libraries have focused their stories on attributes like these and developed compelling messages. However, I generally encourage a library to think at a broader, more emotional level. Think about the needs that patrons have in everyday life and how the library could help

THE STORY

address those needs—and then use attributes as support points that reassure your patrons that you can in fact meet those needs. For example, in today's world it can be very hard for people to find a quiet, peaceful place for contemplation and study. Thus, the library could be defined as a place for rejuvenation—mental, physical, emotional. The library is uniquely suited to fill this role, no other organization has the ability to address this need in the same way (except possibly Starbucks!), and it is obviously something that has relevance to patrons. This message is much more powerful than a listing of the library's quiet study rooms and the number of books in the library's self-help section. The availability of quiet study rooms and a large self-help section can support the notion of rejuvenation, but they lack the gut-level resonance that rejuvenation evokes. If you find that your message starts to look like a laundry list of services that your library offers, it is a warning to stop and rethink. I firmly believe that libraries are uniquely situated to meet some very specific needs in our society. Think carefully about these as you start to develop your message.

Writing a Tagline

Once you have defined your branding message, whether based on your mission/vision or developed independently, you will need to write a tagline. A tagline takes the internal branding message and makes it short, intriguing, and attention-grabbing to potential users of your library.

As a first step in this process you will want to develop a common language for portraying your library and its newly crafted role in your community. Ask your Core Team to get together for a brainstorming session and complete the exercise at the end of this chapter, defining a list of words that everyone agrees describe your library.

Once your Core Team has arrived at a common language for speaking about your brand, it is time to start thinking about a tagline. Bring examples

Frequently Asked Question

My library has a logo. Why do I need a tagline?

If you know your logo tells your brand story without a tagline, then you do not need one. Some logos are visually specific enough to stand on their own. However, if you have any doubts about your logo's ability to tell your brand story—then add a tagline.

of other libraries' taglines to get people going (Boston Public Library—*Books are just the beginning;* West Palm Beach Public Library—*An oasis of knowledge;* Harris County Public Library—*Your pathway to knowledge*).

Start by asking everyone to just call out their ideas for a tagline. Write all of them down, and see if there are any ideas or phrases that get used consistently. Then, consider the words in your common language. Do the taglines use those words? Do they capture the concepts inherent in those words? Is it possible to rephrase some of the suggested taglines using terms from your common language? Then, just as you did when developing your brand message, use a thesaurus to see if you can come up with alternative words that might expand or strengthen your preliminary work. Strive to develop a tagline of no more than five to ten words, keeping in mind that a tagline needs to be very good if it is going to approach ten words. Pick out the top ten ideas and, as before, ask everyone to take them home to get feedback and more ideas from friends and family. At your next meeting, ask your Core Team to boil the ideas down to the top five. Make sure that the team can live with any of those ideas as the final option. Then ask your Board (or library decision makers) to make the final choice. When I did this the first time, the library's board chose an option that was definitely not one of Core Team's favorites. However, we could live with the choice, and the board had very concrete reasons for making that decision. Therefore, in the end everyone was happy.

In Wakefield, once we had determined that our vision of the library's role in the community was as a place where people in the community could connect with each other, with information, with literature, with the world, we asked the staff to think about ways to articulate that via a tagline. The results were amazing—librarians love a challenge like this and within twenty-four hours we had collected over 150 ideas! If you think your staff is too small to generate enough ideas, ask them to take the branding message home and get ideas from family and friends, or send out the concept to friends online and ask them for input. We did all of the above and ended up with over two hundred ideas in our pool. Or you might go to a local school that teaches marketing and ask a professor to use the creation of your tagline as a class exercise to see what the students come up with.

As you define your tagline, it is important to keep in mind that you are specifying what your brand will do for potential users. You are also saying (by implication) that your brand cannot do everything. This is frequently a tough concept for public librarians in particular to understand—we often feel that because we are a free, democratic institution, our branding should be directed toward the world in general. However, the very fact that you are considering branding means that you are planning to tailor your message to specific audiences. Focusing on a specific audience, rather than trying to appeal to everyone, increases the efficiency of your communication. Targeting your message to a specific audience allows you to talk to them one-on-one. Imagine that you are in a crowded room with people from many different backgrounds. You can either try to talk with everyone in the room or communicate with only a small group. In most cases your communication will be more effective if you focus on a small group of individuals who can hear what you are saying, understand the language you are speaking, and relate to the message you are delivering. Targeting your message also allows you to spend your branding funds more effectively. If you had an unlimited amount of money, you could communicate in some fashion with every possible library user. However, I do not know of any libraries that enjoy that kind of funding. Typically, if we have any money at all for branding, the amount is limited and we have to be smart about how we use it. When we concentrate on a small group, we produce only the materials they require, which results in financial efficiency.

Make Sure Your Message Is Honest

For your brand message to be honest, your library must be able to do what you say it is going to do in your message, or it must be taking steps toward delivering on that promise. Never promise something you cannot deliver or are not taking steps to deliver. For example, if your library is an empty shell

Frequently Asked Question

My library has a logo and a tagline, but no one seems to remember them. What can I do about that?

The first thing you need to do is to identify the real problem. Is there poor awareness of your logo and tagline because they have not been marketed and thus people have not seen them very often, or because they are not memorable? Start by looking at how you use your logo and tagline. Do you use them consistently and constantly or only sporadically? If your use is sporadic, try employing them more regularly and then see if awareness builds over time. If that still does not seem to increase awareness, talk with your users (either directly or via a survey). Ask them what the library's brand message is and see if they can articulate it. Ask them if the brand message means anything to them. If users fail to respond appropriately to either question, you need to rethink your message.

on weekends because students have all left campus, do not try to tell students that the library is the campus social center. All you need to do to lose users is to have one individual come into your library expecting a certain experience based on your message—and then not have that experience delivered. The bad thing about unhappy customers is that they go away, but they rarely tell you why. As a result, you start losing users but you do not understand why. In addition, unhappy users tend to tell other users what made them unhappy, and then you can get a chain reaction of folks who are anticipating having a bad experience. Think about when you have purchased a product that did not do what you expected it to do. You were probably annoyed and determined never to purchase that product again. Well, the exact same thing happens with libraries. If you want to develop a message about what your library *will* become, make sure you are taking steps today to move in that direction. This will keep your brand honest and your users happy.

One way to tell whether you are keeping your brand message honest is by whether or not it generates buzz. Buzz is created when one person tells another person about a product or service. Because most people prefer to get references from friends and family about products and services, buzz is a very powerful way of building awareness about a product or service. If you think your library has a strong, honest message and that you are delivering on that message, do not be afraid to ask people to pass that information along. For example, you might have a Pass It on Week in which you ask every patron who comes to your circulation desk to pass on a good word about the library (and a free bookmark or refrigerator sticker) to a friend who might be interested. Or you might ask regular library users if they would be willing to put a positive quote about the library on a library blog. There is nothing wrong with asking, and if you are delivering on your message (being honest), then it is very likely that your library users will respond very positively. As a group libraries and librarians are not particularly good at tooting their own horns. A Pass It on Week is a great way of letting people know how good your organization is—and of having someone else do the tooting!

■ ■ ■ ■

To summarize: Use your brand audit to help you determine if an existing brand message is a good one. You should use your library's mission or vision statement as a starting point for developing a branding message. If your library does not have a mission or vision, then your Core Team will need to determine the basic content of one in order to develop a comprehensive branding message. Once the branding message is defined, the Core Team will need to develop a tagline—a short, concise, and attention-grabbing way of articulating the library's branding message. Regardless of whether you are redefining an existing branding message or defining a new one, you will need to make sure that your brand message is honest—that you do not promise more than your library can deliver.

Exercise

Objective
To develop a common language to describe your library and its role in your community as a preliminary to writing a brand tagline.

Activity
This activity can be done with the library staff, with senior managers, with board members—in short, with any group that is strongly vested in the success of the library.

1. Do some very basic research about your community's future direction. You can collect this information by looking at your town (or college's) comprehensive plan (if it has one), by talking to someone who manages your community's growth and development, or by looking at demographic projections from the U.S. Census Bureau. At a meeting with your Core Team, share this information in a consolidated format. Discuss what you think your community's direction will be over the next five years.

2. Prior to this meeting, write down possible descriptors of your library, one term per three-by-five-inch index card. Then, on more index cards write down the opposite of each term that you originally identified. A list of potential words is included in appendix A to get you going, but you may want to add or subtract words of your own.

3. Have Core Team members work individually or in pairs. Distribute the index cards randomly among the groups. Ask each group to keep the library in mind as they go through the cards quickly. Their task is to identify any words that they think describe your library and its current or possible role in the community and to eliminate any words that they do not find useful. They should spend only ten minutes on this exercise, so they need to rely on first impressions and not spend too much time on the nuances of language.

4. Each team should choose the ten words that they think best describe the library. The objective is to have a maximum of one hundred words as a

starting point. Post all the words in one place and ask the entire group to spend ten minutes reviewing them. At the end of that time period, ask the participants to put a checkmark by each of their three favorite words. The results of this round of voting will help you pare down your original list.

5.   Post a second list that consists of the words that received the most votes in step 4 and ask participants to immediately put one checkmark by their single most favored word. Out of this process, you should arrive at a final list of five to ten words that everyone feels do a good job of describing your library. If your list is still too long, you can ask for a third vote to reduce the number of words one more time. Your goal is to find words that seem right at first glance, without spending a tremendous amount of time debating exact definitions. Ultimately, this exercise depends on gut instinct rather than intellect. The selected words will serve as the common language used to craft a tagline as described in this chapter.

■7■ The Visuals
Attention-Grabbing Support for Your Message

Developing your brand's visual image (your logo and brand design elements) is the part of branding that everyone grasps because logos have been around for a long time and everyone understands why we use them—to identify our brand. However, it can be difficult to get a strong, well-designed logo because frequently someone on the board or staff says, "I have a cousin (niece, nephew) who likes artistic things. Why not let him develop a logo?" And given that such people will usually happily work for free, everyone agrees. The end result is generally a well-meaning but less-than-great logo. Look around—you will see them everywhere. The other thing that can happen is that a logo is developed at one point in time and the brand's messaging developed at another point. The end result is two brand elements that have no relationship to each other and do not really make sense when considered together. Examples of such lack of coherence can also be easily found.

Finding a Designer

When faced with the need to design your library's visual image, you may be tempted to roll your eyes and say, "I can't do this; I don't know any graphic designers and my library doesn't have the money to hire one." Do not despair. You can still develop a top-notch brand logo and design elements. You just need to get creative about where you can get help. The following are some ideas to explore:

1. If you are part of a school or university community or have one nearby, call their art department and ask if they can recommend a graphic design student that might be interested in doing the work (for free or for minimal

payment) to build her portfolio. Or ask if you could talk with a professor who might be interested in doing the design work as part of a class project.

2. If you do not have a college or university nearby, consider going to your local high school and ask if you could post a notice on bulletin boards—both electronic and hard copy. Talk to teachers/professors and see if this might be a project for a semester. Or you could offer to have a contest for students, the prize being the use of the winning logo on all the library's branding materials. Although high school students might not have the experience or background of a professional designer, they do have tremendous energy, enthusiasm, and creativity. Also, you could develop a very strong public relations program around the contest that would give your library, the school, and the winning student lots of good exposure. That can do a lot to make up for a less-than-perfect logo. If you do use students, just remember to be very clear about what you do and do not want. Your creative brief (described later in this chapter) will be even more important with this group because they will not be as used to following specifications as a professional designer would be. Therefore, you will need to be very clear in spelling out your expectations and desires.

3. Look around your community and identify businesses or nonprofits that have logos that you like. Call those organizations and ask who did the work. Once you have several designers identified, call them, explain the project, and see if one might be willing to do the work pro bono or for a reduced fee. Frequently, large companies will undertake or subsidize such projects as a way of giving back to a community—and libraries are a popular cause.

4. Do a search online that includes the terms *logo, brand, design, small business,* or *nonprofit* along with the name of your community. Frequently you can find small, independent designers who will work on a project basis. Also, there are many websites today that connect design buyers with design sellers. The prices are often very reasonable because the designers are young, starting out, and trying to build a portfolio. You might find that your preferred designer lives far away, but as long as you can communicate via e-mail, the end results will usually be of good quality. If you decide to go this route, ask to see samples of the designer's prior work. Also, keep in mind that any imagery the designer might use in the logo will not be original (meaning she did not draw the image herself). Instead, the image will most likely come from an image book (a compendium of images that are not copyrighted and can be used by anyone). This generally is not a huge issue for libraries, but you do have to consider that you might end up seeing a key element of your prized logo being used by some other library across the country.

5. Finally, ask around. You never know when a family member or friend might have run into a good designer through a community theater or PTA

project. Additionally, do not forget to talk to your staff. Given the number of people going into librarianship as a second or third career, it is very possible that you might find that one of your staff members was a graphic designer in a former life. If so, he might be willing to put his skills to work again for the sake of the library.

Just a note: You might be tempted to develop a logo on your own. If you have some sort of background in graphic design or art, then by all means do so. If you do not, then I would strongly suggest that you find someone to help you with this part of the process. Unless you have the eye of a creative person, it is very difficult to come up with creative, arresting, unique designs. Think carefully about your own skill sets and then act accordingly.

When you do find a designer (or several possible designers), there are a number of things you should do before agreeing to work together. You should start by asking to see the person's portfolio. A portfolio is a compilation of an artist's work. As you look at the portfolio, listen to your gut instinct. Do you like what you see or parts of what you see? If not, walk away immediately. Design work is so subjective that if you do not like an artist's basic style, nothing can be done to change that. Assuming that you do like the portfolio, ask if you might speak to one or two people with whom the person has worked. If your candidate is a student, ask if you can talk with a teacher or professor. This is essentially a simple reference check to see if the individual is trustworthy and can be depended on to deliver your product on time. Next, make sure you have spent enough time with the person to know you can work with him. If you are very timetable oriented and your candidate is very creative and relaxed about timetables, either you are going to have to adjust (because the designer probably will not) or the two of you will have to come to some understanding about how you will work together. Finally, if all looks good, have an open and honest discussion about payment for the project. Explain exactly what you can and cannot afford to pay. Do not forget to identify money needed to print materials (if that is part of the project) and money designated to pay a designer for the creative work.

If you do have money to pay a professional designer, make sure you understand whether or not each candidate has done prior brand identity or logo work. Graphic designers specialize in various areas (just like doctors), and if possible you want someone who regularly designs logos rather than packaging, magazine ads, or something else. It takes a special skill to understand an organization and then visually represent it via a logo, so if you are going to pay for the service, you might as well get the best you can afford.

Writing a Creative Brief

A creative brief is a one-page document that puts in writing all the key information you want the designer to know before starting the project. It is an important way of initiating clear communication. Because design work is an artistic process, it can be very subjective. Consequently, it is very easy for a designer to go off-path. A creative brief is a simple way of defining the parameters of the project, of saying what is and is not acceptable in the end result. In short, it sets the ground rules between the library and the designer so that they both agree on the timing, process, and desired outcome of the work. If you do not start with a creative brief, you are at risk of running into misunderstandings and confusion very early on in the process. A creative brief is invaluable whether you are developing a completely new brand or revising an existing brand.

The first component of a creative brief should be the articulation of the *objective* of the project, for example, to develop a new brand logo or to revise an existing logo for use in all branding materials, or to develop an updated logo that will better reflect the library's current status in its community, or to develop a revised logo that will fix several small design concerns. The objective will tell the designer very clearly what you want to have happen as a result of the project. Your definition of success should focus on having that objective achieved.

As part of the objective you should also identify specific *deliverables*. Deliverables are the actual things that you should have in hand at the end of the project. You might want a color logo and a black-and-white logo in JPEG and PDF formats. You might want a logo that includes the library's tagline. You might want a logo and other design elements to be used in branding materials. You might want design standards (a statement of all of the branding elements and how they should be used). It is up to you to articulate exactly what you expect to get at the end of the project. Do not expect to get anything more or less than what you define. I try to be very careful about this part of the creative brief because what I identify as deliverables will strongly influence the cost of the project. If you find that you have left something out, then expect to pay for adding it at a later date.

The creative brief should also identify the *use* of the new design work. For example, the new logo will be used on all library promotional materials, letterhead, and book bags; it will not be used on signage. This helps the designer understand the contexts in which the logo will be put to work and identify any related constraints. It also helps the designer anticipate the need to develop variations of the logo. For example, some retail stores have both vertically and horizontally oriented logos to fit on signs of various sizes.

A word of caution: Before you talk to the designer about the use of the logo, think about whether your in-house staff will be able to adapt the logo as new needs arise or you will depend on the designer to make adaptations. If you think the work will be done in-house, make sure to tell the designer that you need a print-ready copy of the logo. That should not be a problem given that most design work is done on computers anyway. If you are willing to have the designer manage production of new stationery, business cards, and the like, it is not as critical for you to have a print-ready copy of the logo.

Next, the creative brief should tell the designer anything about the work that *must* or *must not* happen—what I call *absolutes*. For example, if you already know that the colors you want are sky blue and earth brown and that the Arial typeface must not be used, then you need to specify that. Such disclosures are important because when a designer presents you with a preliminary sketch of a lavender logo, it is unfair to suddenly say, "Oh, I forgot to tell you that we can't use lavender in the logo." If you want to use some component of an existing logo, this is where you identify that. When we started revising the logo at Wakefield, the director felt strongly about keeping the beehive that had been part of the original logo. She had spent a lot of time and energy finding that drawing, felt it was appropriate to the library, and wanted to make sure any new logo incorporated it. This was spelled out for the designer in the creative brief before we ever started revising the library's logo.

In addition, the library's branding *message* needs to be clearly stated. Given that the message, tagline, and logo all need to be closely coordinated, the message and tagline must be determined and the designer must understand them before work on the logo can start.

Finally, do not forget to put in a basic *timetable*. It will be up to the designer to come back to you with a detailed timetable. If you have a specific *budget* you should also put that into the creative brief.

Optionally, you might want to put into your creative brief *examples* of work you like or dislike. This can help a designer understand what does or does not resonate with you. If you do this, make sure that you articulate as best you can what you do or do not like. For example, you might say that you do not like the colors in a specific logo because they are too garish or that you do not like a design because it is too modern (or too dated). If you cannot explain why you like or dislike something, then do not share it with the designer because it will not be helpful.

I would suggest that you, as project leader, write the creative brief but then ask your Core Team to respond to it. Have you missed anything? Do they understand what you want from this project? They will help to ensure that your creative brief is simple and easy to understand.

Working with the Designer

After you have developed a creative brief, sit down with your potential designer and go through it carefully. Make sure he understands all of the elements and give him plenty of opportunity for questions. Be willing to make adjustments if you hear a good idea. This should be a collaborative process that you both can feel good about.

Once you have reviewed the brief, if the designer is interested in doing the work, ask him to write a very simple, short proposal for you. In the proposal, the designer should state how many meetings and revisions will be expected. Keep in mind that you cannot make infinite adjustments to creative work without paying for the process. So if you know that you are good at making quick decisions, you might feel that you will need only an initial meeting to review three logo options and one follow-up meeting to review revisions to the chosen logo design. If you are not as good at making quick decisions, you might tell the designer that you need to see five preliminary designs from which you will chose one design. Then you will need three meetings to go through revisions of that chosen design. If you do not specify these details with a designer, most will come to you with one design and expect you to love it. So do yourself a favor and be honest with yourself about how you think you will need to work through the process. Also, if you have asked for five preliminary designs and three follow-up meetings and the cost is too high, consider cutting back on the number of designs and meetings. That should bring your project price down immediately. Also remember that phone calls use the designer's time. You should not agree to two meetings and then think that you can have additional discussions on the phone. Many designers see a long phone discussion as another meeting and they will charge you accordingly. E-mails are about the only type of communication that does not cost extra money and that is because the designer can manage the process of responding to e-mails.

Who should be at your working meetings with your designer? I would include one or two members of my Core Team but probably no more. Why

Tip

Being a designer is not an easy job. A designer tries to translate an intellectual concept into a visual representation. As you give feedback to a designer, try to be fair and friendly. Doing so will make life much happier for the designer and will probably improve communications as you go through the project.

not? Again, design is a very subjective process. Designers tend to be sensitive about their work—it is a creative expression for them. If you get too many people in the room, it is too easy for the conversation to turn into "I like this," "I don't like this," without any concrete, useful feedback for the designer to consider. A smaller group tends to think more carefully about their input and how it is being received by the designer. However, after the meeting with the designer, I would certainly share the outcome with your Core Team and possibly your Support Team to ensure that they continue to feel part of the branding process.

When you have your first meeting with your designer to review the preliminary logos, the work of the meeting is up to the designer. He should begin by walking through the creative brief to recap the parameters of the project. If he does not, you might want to do so. Then the designer will present all of the preliminary logos he has prepared (generally between one and five, depending on what you have negotiated). I would suggest that you ask the designer to go through all the options while you listen but withhold comment. The designer will give you his thoughts on why each choice meets the criteria you identified in your creative brief. As the designer is speaking, take notes to yourself about questions, likes, and dislikes. The reason I advise looking at all the options before commenting is that sometimes it is easier to figure out what is and is not appealing by comparing one design to another.

When having a discussion with a designer, I go through the following steps:

1. Once the designer is finished presenting, I always tell her I appreciate her work. I say this regardless of how good or bad that work is.

2. I identify the designs that I particularly like and then tell the designer what I like about them, such as that the colors are good or that the design is elegant and works with the message.

3. I am as concrete as possible about things I do not like about the designs, such as that typeface feels too young or that the logo does not seem to work with the brand's message. I usually do not say "I don't like that" without offering a concrete reason. If you are not specific, it is impossible for the designer to make effective changes because she cannot read your mind.

4. I answer any questions the designer might have for me.

If I have a one or two favorite preliminary designs, I tell the designer to focus on those. However, I do *not* at any time tell the designer what to change or how to change it. My secret to getting good design work is to let the designer do her job. This means I tell her my likes and dislikes but then I leave it up to her to figure out how to make changes that will address my concerns.

Doing otherwise gives the impression that the client is trying to become the designer, and nothing will make a real designer crazy faster than this! Plus, it is very unlikely that you will find as good an answer to your concerns as the designer will. So you do your job and let the designer do hers.

The designer will listen to your input and go away to make adjustments. At the next meeting, take off your analytical cap and put on your intuitive cap. As soon as the designer shows you the next revision of the logo, respond to it quickly at the gut level. Is it working or not? If it is working, then go back and analyze it to see if there is anything missing. However, do not analyze the details to death. This is the point at which you should start reacting at an emotional level to the designer's work. If you have specific input (and your agreement includes additional revisions), the designer will take your input, go away to make changes, and then come back to you again. Once you have gone through your revisions and have a brand logo that you like, you are ready to start using the final product. As mentioned earlier, make sure that the designer supplies you a print-ready PDF or other file format of the logo for future use.

Sometimes designers offer to help with the printing of whatever materials you might be producing with the new brand. This means that they will go to the print shop and review the first prints that are produced to ensure that colors and placement are right. I would suggest accepting any designer's offer to do this. It ensures that the printer will do the job correctly and that your final product will be of good quality. Otherwise, you should be willing to go to the print shop yourself to make sure you are happy with the product before large quantities are produced.

■ ■ ■ ■

To summarize: There are many sources of free or inexpensive help with the design of your brand logo, including colleges, high schools, online sites, and pro bono help from professional design firms. To work with a designer you will need to develop a creative brief that outlines your project objective, the uses of the design work, your design absolutes, the library's message, a project timetable, a budget, and, if possible, examples of logos that you like. You will then need to walk your designer through the creative brief before the work begins. When you see your designer's preliminary logos, do not be afraid to say what you like as well as dislike and to give the designer a chance to ask you questions. Be clear about your expectations at every meeting, but also be willing to adjust if your designer comes up with a great idea that is slightly outside the parameters of what you had been considering.

Exercise

Objective

To develop the branding project manager's understanding of how to give effective feedback to a graphic designer.

Activity

1. This is a role-playing exercise. Find a partner with whom you can work on this activity. Your partner will play the part of a brand graphic designer.

2. Write your creative brief. Then sit down with your partner and go through it. At the end of the process ask your partner to repeat the most important points that he heard you say. If your partner did not hear all of the key information, go back and rethink how you might present the logo-related part of the creative brief more effectively.

3. Make a copy of any library's branding materials. (You can pull a copy from the Internet.) With your partner still playing the role of the designer, assume that he has just presented the sample branding materials to you. Using concrete, specific examples, explain the following to your designer:

   a. What you like about the materials
   b. What you do not like about the materials
   c. What you think is missing

   Ask your designer for feedback about what you said. Ask if your feedback was concrete, for example, "This blue color is too dark and dull; it needs to be energized and exciting." Ask if he could walk away from the interview with a good understanding of how the design needs to be changed. If he cannot give good feedback to you, then again review what you said and consider how you might be more specific and less subjective.

■8■ Brand Standards, Brand Advocates, and Marketing

You have done a brand audit so you know where your brand stands today. You have done the work to define what you want your brand message and visual identity to be in the future. All the elements have been put together into an effective and interesting brand. Now it is time to start using your new brand effectively.

Your first step is to get everyone in your library using the brand. This means your Core and Support teams as well as your entire staff. A good way of facilitating this process is to develop a formal set of written standards for the brand. Standards come in two forms—editorial and design. Editorial standards are guidelines for writing about your brand, and design standards are guidelines for using the visual components of your brand, such as the logo and brand colors.

Editorial Standards

Editorial standards identify all of the key rules for how your staff and key stakeholders will talk about the brand in writing. The brand's message as defined internally is spelled out, as are the occasions for its use. The brand attributes that support your brand message are also spelled out. Similarly, the tagline is defined as well as the occasions for its use. Finally, any specific editorial points are included. For example, the following are some editorial guidelines for the Lucius Beebe Memorial Library:

- *Library* should not be capitalized unless it is being used as a proper noun (the Beebe Library).
- However, job titles, department names, and room names should be capitalized (Circulation Office, Reference).

- Every publication must include the library logo and contact information.

Your guidelines should be written down and compiled into one document. It can be difficult to persuade library staff to follow editorial guidelines. They tend to forget the rules (or ignore them), and they have to be reminded on a fairly regular basis about their use. The document is more likely to be used if it is short and concise. Try to focus only on the most important editorial content. Then lead all affected staff and board members through a brief training session to help them understand how to use the guidelines and why it is important to do so. They will be the ones doing most of the branding work, so they must be the starting point for consistency of approach.

Design Standards

After editorial guidelines are developed, design guidelines should be prepared. They do the same thing for the brand's design that the editorial guidelines do brand-related writing. They identify the basic rules of how the various visual elements should be used.

Begin by defining what the logo looks like and how it is used. Include any and all variations. What size should the logo be? Are there both horizontal and vertical versions of the logo? Is the brand's tagline always used with the logo, or can the logo stand on its own? Additionally, identify any other design elements that are acceptable (page borders, decorative elements, etc.) and how to use them.

Identify any and all color variations of the logo that are acceptable. Ten years ago the logo would have been available in one format and that would have been it. Today the use of visual elements is much more flexible. Frequently a logo may appear in a variety of colors or combinations of colors.

Specify the logo's placement on written and printed materials. On stationery, signs, business cards, and the like, will the logo be found centered at the bottom, in the upper right hand corner, or somewhere else?

Design standards are not developed to curtail creativity. They are developed to ensure that everyone understands what is and is not acceptable when using the library's logo. Generally, people can be as creative as desired as long as they understand the few rules that must be followed.

Once your design standards are developed, everyone in your library should be trained to understand their use. In Wakefield, to simplify the process, we asked the designer with whom we worked to develop what we called brand templates. A template is a sample product (such as a bookmark) that holds certain design elements constant (such as the color and placement of the logo) but allows the content and certain other components to be changed to fit the needs of specific events. We developed templates for the basic materials that we produced most often—bookmarks and promotional flyers. The templates were designed in Microsoft Publisher, which was available on all of the library staff computers. This meant that after initial training, any staff member could use a template to develop their own promotional materials for specific events. In this way the entire staff became owners of the branding process: they could make creative changes within the template's constraints. The library's brand advocate was available when staff members had questions about ideas they had for the templates.

There are several positives to developing templates. They allow the library to develop marketing materials without having to go back to a designer every time something new is needed. In addition, they allow a library to produce materials much more inexpensively—for example, we were able to print our bookmarks and flyers in color at the library. They also ensure that staff members can be creative within the specific constraints of brand standards. Providing editorial and design standards along with brand templates is a very effective way of moving branding into the heart of an organization.

The Brand Advocate

Another step in promoting brand consciousness within the library is to select a member of your staff to be the brand advocate. The job of the brand advocate is to oversee how the brand is being developed and used in the library, to identify situations in which the brand is not being used appropriately or with consistency, and to identify positive evolutions of the brand that the library might want to incorporate into its vision. Libraries should decide for themselves how they might want this role to work. One of the following models might be appropriate:

(!) Tip

The best brand advocates are individuals who are passionate about branding and understand its power but are also able to understand how others might feel conflicted about using a business tool in a nonprofit environment. People who have an urgent need to be right on a regular basis rarely make good brand advocates.

1. The brand advocate as general overseer. The brand advocate's responsibility is to look at all branding materials that go out. When there are substantial deviations from the editorial or design standards, the brand advocate discusses them with the staff member that developed the materials. Together, they decide what is appropriate and make changes as necessary. This role will usually work well in smaller libraries where all staff members know each other and are used to working together in a collegial environment.

2. The brand advocate as final arbiter. In this scenario the brand advocate has final approval over all marketing materials that leave the library. This person decides whether materials meet brand standards and can make changes as necessary to ensure compliance with the standards. This model will be more appropriate in larger libraries where there is a real need to have one specialist ensuring that everything that goes out of the library meets brand standards, lest the multitude of materials start to create a multiplicity of brand looks.

3. The brand advocate as teacher/trainer. In this model the brand advocate is the acknowledged branding expert whose job is to train staff about branding and to help them understand what does and does not work within a branding environment. This model can work in either a small or a large library, but it is important that the individual chosen as the brand advocate enjoys teaching and is able to guide without dictating.

Whichever of these models is used, the brand advocate needs to have a real interest in branding and its use in the organization. Some helpful traits are passion about the concept of branding and its usefulness in a library, creativity, and a willingness to learn a new set of skills not traditionally thought of as important for a librarian. Generally, I have found that branding is adopted most smoothly when the staff is a core component of the development process and receives training to ensure that they understand why branding is important and how it will be used. A brand advocate should be

Tip

Brand advocates have to have the strength of their convictions. They need to maintain consistency in how the library's brand is used, which requires the ability (and power) to speak diplomatically with colleagues who fail to follow brand standards.

able to articulate those points quickly and easily and act as a promoter for the branding concept in the organization.

The Transition to a New Brand

An important step in the transition from old to new is to develop a timetable for working through old branding materials so that new branding materials can start to be printed and used in the organization. There are very few libraries with enough funding to simply toss out all their old materials (business cards, letterhead, signage, promotional pieces, posters, flyers) and start over with their new brand. My recommendation is to develop a timetable for using up as many of the old materials as possible and gradually phasing in the new ones. To do this you will need a careful inventory of what branding materials you have and how much there is of each one. Estimate how long each type of material will last and when you can start buying new materials with the new brand. You may discover that it will take you two years to go through your stationery, but everything else will be ready to change over in six months. In that case you may want to consider changing to the new stationery sooner to ensure that at some point (ideally no further out than a year from the start of work) all of your branding materials will be in place.

Creating a Marketing Plan

Once you have gone through your promotional materials and identified how you will transition to your new or revised brand, you might want to consider developing a marketing plan for your library. A marketing plan identifies across the period of a year what library activities will need some sort of promotion. In a public library, a marketing plan is a good idea because it helps make sure that adult activities and children's activities are not conflicting with each other and that the library has a plan for how it is going to promote all programs. In an academic library a marketing plan can help ensure that the library is getting out into the academic community to promote itself and what it offers. In either type of library a marketing plan also ensures that the library is consistent in its efforts to reach its target audience and in the delivery of its brand message. A simple marketing plan can be made up by taking the following steps:

- Identify your target audience (see chapter 1).
- Compile a one-year timetable of activities you will be having in your library to reach that audience.

- Identify the marketing tools you will use to promote each activity, such as bookmarks, flyers, presentations, posters, or radio announcements.
- Put together a budget for developing each promotional piece.
- Identify roles and responsibilities for getting each promotional piece done.

Put it all together and your marketing plan is done! A marketing plan can be as simple or sophisticated as desired. My recommendation is that if you have never done one before, keep your first one simple by following the steps outlined above. Then share your marketing plan with your entire staff and keep it available as a reference tool throughout the year.

■ ■ ■ ■

To summarize: There are several helpful tools that can be used to facilitate the use of branding in a library. Libraries can develop editorial standards that define how to write about the library. They can also develop design standards that articulate how to use the visual components of a brand, such as its logo, its colors, and its font. Standard templates can be developed that hold some design components consistent while allowing staff to change other components as usage dictates. Finally, it is helpful to appoint a brand advocate to promote and oversee branding within the library. It will be this individual's responsibility to manage the concept of branding to maximize its advantages for the library.

Exercise

Objective
To help drive home the need for editorial standards and brand standards.

Activity
By e-mail ask everyone on your Core Team to write a short paragraph that describes the work of one or two departments in the library and includes an example of the library's branding. Print each answer on a separate sheet of paper, staple the pages together, and share with the Core Team at a training meeting. The most likely outcome of this exercise is that the team will see no consistency in how the library is described (is it "The Library" or "the library" or "the Curtis Memorial Library" or "Curtis"?) or in how the brand is represented (is the logo in color, in black and white, with a tagline, or without?). Discuss how editorial and design standards will help address this issue and, depending on the makeup of your Core Team, ask for their help in convincing the library staff as a whole that brand standards are crucial.

▪9▪   How to Work with Outside Help

There are several places in a branding project where you might bring in outside help if your library has funds to do so. Your library might hire a marketing consultant to help you develop your brand message. You might hire a graphic designer to help you work on the library's visual identity. You might hire a consultant to manage the entire project for you. The information in this chapter will assist you in deciding if you need help with a branding project and provide some guidelines for hiring and managing outside help.

How to Decide If You Need Help

A branding project consists of the following activities: developing the library's message, developing the library's visual components (the logo), implementing use of the brand throughout the library organization, and evaluating the success of the branding effort. As mentioned earlier in this book, all of these tasks can be performed by in-house staff if necessary. However, if there are any extra funds available, I would definitely suggest getting outside help to do the design work. There is a creative component to this work that is truly wonderful when done by a competent professional. I believe smart amateurs can do everything else in this book. However, the following key questions will help you decide how much of the work in a branding project you can or want to tackle:

1. Are there any funds available for hiring outside help? If not, are you willing to put the time and effort into writing a grant proposal to get funding? If your answer to both questions is no, you will need to figure out how

you will accomplish the branding project on your own. It can be done; you will just need patience and energy to carry it through. I will provide some tips further on for people who have to do the project all by themselves.

2. Do you have any experience at all with marketing or branding? If not, do you have the time to do a little self-training? If you lack experience and do not have time to do any reading, then you will probably need some professional help and guidance.

3. Do you know of anyone that can help you with this project on a regular basis? It does not have to be a staff member; it can just as easily be a library volunteer. The key is that the person must be willing to provide regular help that you can plan on. If you can count on a staff member or volunteer to share the workload, you are likely to need less hired help.

4. Do you have senior support for the branding project within your library? If that support is lukewarm, you might consider hiring outside help simply because outsiders (sadly) are given a level of credibility that is not always accorded to staff. Hiring an experienced consultant to help with your project and present to your board is often a great way of selling the concept of branding. On the other hand, if you have strong support for your branding project, you can probably decide if you want outside help—your board will probably do whatever is necessary to ensure your success.

5. Finally, you, as the project leader, should honestly evaluate your own commitment to the branding project. Starting something new (which branding is to most organizations) is never easy. You will need to put great personal energy and enthusiasm into the branding process to make it work in your library. If for any reason you lack the excitement necessary to bring the project to fruition, then I would strongly recommend bringing in outside help. There is no point starting the project if you do not have the personal energy to see it through to the end.

General Guidelines

The information in this section builds on the discussion at the beginning of chapter 7 about how to find free or inexpensive help with your branding work and how to evaluate the skills of candidates for the job of your brand's designer.

Keep in mind whenever you work with outside help that you (the project manager) are the expert. You know your library and the members of your various teams better than any person whom you might hire to help you. I always emphasize this point because sometimes it is too easy to be swayed by a very knowledgeable and smart consultant. You should *never* allow yourself to be talked into doing something that does not really make sense for your library. Be guided by what experts tell you, but if a suggestion does not feel right, do not act on it. Your instinct is telling you something and you should trust it. Do not feel insecure about your level of expertise—you have been asked to do this project because someone feels you have the capability.

It is generally helpful to have a frank conversation with anyone you are hiring to help with the branding work. Explain your philosophy of working with consultants. That should be something like "You are the expert. We want and are looking forward to your help and input, but ultimately, at the end of the day, I'm the one who will make the final decisions about what will and won't work for the library." This can be done very pleasantly and professionally and is actually very helpful to anyone that you hire because it establishes the parameters of their authority within the project.

Do not assume that your library is unimportant because you do not have a big budget. Do not be afraid to ask a firm if they do pro bono work. You might wonder why a professional firm would want to work for your library for free. But, in fact, most agencies (if they do pro bono work at all) are usually happy to consider a project for a local library because libraries tend to be held in such high esteem by the general public. Any work they do for a library more than pays for itself in terms of reflected positive appeal. As added incentive, you might tell the firm that you will build an extensive public relations campaign around the work when it is finished. Most local papers gladly give space to newsworthy local library stories, and this is a great way for a firm to get its name out in a community.

But then again, never assume that you are the most important client a firm will have. When you are getting work done for a reduced rate or for free, you have to be willing to take a backseat to paying clients. Assume things will take longer than you might want. Consultants typically have multiple clients at any one time. The biggest clients have to be taken care of first because they are the ones who pay the bills. Just make sure to build a little leeway into your timetables to compensate for the fact that your consultant cannot give you uninterrupted attention. Also, although a firm might do the library the courtesy of sending a senior staff member to an initial meeting about the project, do not be surprised if the actual work is done by a more junior staff member. This does not mean you are getting lower quality, it just means you are getting someone who is less experienced. You may also get a more junior person because the firm may bring in people specifically to work on your library's project. I would not be concerned if this happens because less-experienced staff members often bring fresh creativity and enthusiasm to projects that their more experienced partners may have lost. As you are talking with a firm, do not be afraid to ask who will actually be working on the project. If you think it is important, ask to meet that individual.

Do not underestimate the ability of your staff to help with branding work. It frequently amazes me how often a group of librarians can come up with really inventive, intriguing ideas when they understand and support what a branding team is trying to do. Tap into your staff as a key resource. Many of them will probably enjoy the challenge and have fun with the work because it is new and creative. Likewise, many people today are librarians as a second or even third career. One of your staff members might have directly relevant experience to contribute. You just never know where you will find talent, but generally you have to do a little snooping to uncover it.

Let the people you hire do their work. If you do decide to hire outside help, let them do their jobs. This may seem obvious, but for some reason it is very hard for people to take to heart. It is crucial to tell your consultant exactly what you want him to deliver to you as his component of the branding project. If, for example, you are hiring a consultant to help you train your staff in branding and how to use your new brand, say, "I want three training sessions for my entire staff. At the end of the process I want my staff to feel energized, enthusiastic, and knowledgeable about branding." Then let the consultant do his job. Do not try to tell the consultant how to go about providing what you want. For example, do not say, "I want the training sessions to be forty-five minutes long, you need to use PowerPoint presentations, and I don't want my staff to do any role-playing." If you take such an approach, you in essence become the consultant, or at a minimum you tell the consultant how to do his job. Plus such behavior is incredibly annoying, and you will find that people will get less and less interested in being involved in the project. Being an outsider brought in to help with a project can be difficult because everyone has opinions about how the work should be done. The key to success in such an environment is to spell out expectations very clearly at the beginning of the project and then trust the people that you have hired to do the work you want.

Put your ego aside. You have made the decision to go outside your library for help because you have decided that outside experts can provide what you need for your branding project. So let them help you. Accept the fact that there are many ways to get to a great final result. Relax and consider carefully if another person's way might be at least as good as yours and possibly even better.

Before You Hire Anyone

Before you hire outside support, have several staff members meet the potential candidates. Generally, libraries work in a collegial fashion. There are several people involved in a project and they tend to make decisions together. It makes sense to have several people meet any potential outside suppliers because you want to make sure that the new people you bring in can be effective across the organization. If a staff member has a real issue with a particular outside resource, then consider finding another source of help. Never feel that there is only one person or firm that can help you with your branding project. Consultants work hard to make themselves indispensable to their clients because long-term relationships are good for their pocketbooks. However, you should never feel that you are locked into a relationship that is not working for you. You can *always* find another consultant or graphic designer.

Always ask for a written proposal from a potential partner in the branding work. I always ask for a proposal, even if I'm working with a high school student. Sometimes it is very tempting in informal relationships (like those you would tend to have with a student) not to bother with a proposal. However, I think it is important to have one because it spells out the work an individual plans to do and the cost for that work. It is another way (in addition to the creative brief) to ensure that you and your outside help are on the same path with the same plan of action in mind. It ensures that even if a firm is doing the work for your library for free, everyone has the same strategy for getting that work done.

Check references. Always ask for references and always check references. Do not be afraid to ask hard questions when you call the references. Some good questions to consider asking include the following:

- Were you happy with the end product of your project with this individual/firm? Did they deliver what you wanted done?

- Did you have any issues as you went along? How did those issues get resolved? Is there anything you would suggest that I need to be aware of in the work process?

- What would you say this person's work style is? (It is very important that you feel comfortable working with your outside help. You will be involved in a short, intense burst of activity with that person and you want to make sure that you do not get on each other's nerves and end up hating each other at the end of the project.)

- Is there anything else you think I should know about working with this individual/company?

Because the library world is small and quite friendly, I also tend to ask colleagues if they know the person or firm I am considering or if they have heard anything about them. Sometimes you will get more information that way than through formal references.

After You Hire Someone—Setting Expectations

Make sure you clearly define what you expect to be delivered to you at the end of a project. Expectations should be defined before anyone is hired. However, it cannot hurt to verbalize them again after someone is hired. Avoid assuming anything. You cannot go wrong by being annoyingly clear and detailed and it will make everyone's life simpler to understand exactly what is expected.

Look for the not-so-obvious costs. Outside consultants and designers generally are as honest as the next person. They want to do good work because they build their business on referrals. Their goal is to make you happy, not to take your money unreasonably. However, they also need to maximize each consulting engagement that they have because if they do not work, they do not get paid. Therefore, some independent consultants will build costs into a contract in places you might not expect. For example, they might say that they can go over estimated costs by 10 percent before they have to ask your permission, they might charge extra for color copies, or they might charge for mileage to meetings. All of these are reasonable business expenses, but you want to know that they will be charged before you have to pay for them.

 Suggestion for Success

Keep the process moving

Keeping the process moving is similar to not striving for perfection. You do not want to let the process get bogged down in questions or reviews or revisions because it will become far too easy never to start up again. Stalling is a time-honored method of avoiding making decisions or killing a project you do not like. Before you start set very clear timetables that define expectations for involvement. If those do not work and your project starts to lose momentum, make critical decisions yourself. Remember, it really is better to ask forgiveness than permission.

You also want to decide if such charges are reasonable. Therefore, take the time to read the small print in a contract before you sign it. If your library is like most libraries, you probably have a small, very limited budget, so you need to make sure your outside help understands that you absolutely cannot spend anything more than the stipulated amount. If a consultant or designer is used to working with nonprofits, they will understand this limitation. If they have not worked with a nonprofit before, they may have the attitude (which more commonly exists in large corporations) that you can always find the money somewhere. You should make it very clear that it is part of the outside supplier's job to help ensure that you do not go over budget.

Do not be afraid to achieve less-than-perfect results. Many librarians that I have talked to say that they are afraid of branding because they do not know enough and will not come up with a good enough end result. I think it is OK not to be perfect or not to get it all done the first time around. Because branding is such a new tool for libraries, my perspective is that it is more important to do it than to do it perfectly. Get a branding process going— and you can always make revisions in the future if it turns out to be less than perfect. I advise against making a lot of changes to a brand on a regular basis simply because it means your users or customers are always trying to readjust to the new brand. However, I think small changes are not noticed by users, so you can make them as you go along and not risk any major issues.

The Money

It can be difficult to decide whether to tell a potential outside consultant how much you have to spend on her portion of the branding project before you get her proposal. I have a tough time with this situation and it always comes up. I find it amazing how often a proposal from a consultant will come in at $4,995 when I have told him that I have $5,000 to spend. On the other hand, there is no sense in asking someone to spend time developing a project outline if you must ultimately tell him that his plan will cost far more money than you have. So my compromise is that I usually give outside suppliers a range that I would like them to stay within, and I make the high end of the range the most that I can afford to spend. You will still get proposals at the high end of the range (everyone knows how this game is played), but at least you are asking for some careful thought about the proposal.

Check your invoices against your project proposal to make sure you are getting charged what you had planned to get charged. Everyone makes mistakes, but you do not want anyone to make mistakes with your small budget.

If you have questions, do not be afraid to ask. If you do not agree with a charge, request an adjustment. Your supplier might or might not be willing to compromise, but if you do not ask, you will never know. If you are confused about a charge, keep asking questions until you understand it. Keep in mind that this is not your money you are spending and that you have a fiduciary responsibility to make sure it is spent appropriately and reasonably.

Always limit your financial exposure to small increments as you go through the project. In other words, make arrangements to pay your outside help for pieces of the project as they are completed rather than paying up front or waiting until the end to pay a lump sum. When I was a consultant, I would typically ask clients to pay a small amount up front to cover my initial start-up costs (research, materials, etc.). I would then ask for payments when the project was halfway done, when it was about three quarters of the way done, and at the end, when everyone was happy with the conclusion of the project. This approach usually works out well for both the library and the outside help. If you do not like the way the project is progressing, you can stop and not lose all of your money. In addition, most consultants appreciate getting paid for segments of work instead of having to wait until the end of the project, so you have a good solution all around.

Other Thoughts

Look at what other libraries have done—and ask them who did their work. I have done this several times and have never gotten a bad recommendation. If I see a website or a brochure that I like, I always ask who did the work so that I can build up a list of people to go to if I need similar work done. Librarians are wonderful at passing along a good resource, and they will generally be very honest with you about the positives and negatives of that resource.

Read. It seems a little odd to say that to what is probably an audience of librarians. However, what I mean here is do not be afraid to read books about marketing and branding. Reading business books is not the favorite activity of many librarians (unless business is their area of expertise), and many may not see the value of such reading. My theory is that the business world comes up with a lot of great ideas that are easily transferable to libraries. When I am trying to learn something new about marketing or branding, I can almost always do so by finding the newest books on the topic and giving them a quick review. Likewise, there are several websites I find very useful. The ones I go to most regularly include MarketingProfs (www.marketingprofs.com) and Marketing Reveries (www.reveries.com).

Build relationships. Pick three or four marketing blogs or websites that offer content you find useful. Then stick with them. Because these sites want you to come back, they change content frequently and are very helpful in keeping up with the latest news about marketing. You can also e-mail the frequent contributors to ask them questions and request recommendations for outside help. It is amazing how helpful and supportive the Internet community can be—take advantage of it. Also, there are more and more librarians that are investigating and getting into marketing and branding. If you work in a public library, you might consider checking with your library district or county to learn what support they might offer to libraries interested in marketing and branding.

Go to training seminars. Sometimes we forget how many reasonably priced training options are available today. Seek them out and take advantage of them—they are a great learning resource. Do not forget online resources like WebJunction (www.webjunction.org). Their courses are usually affordable, and the time commitment is flexible and manageable.

■ ■ ■ ■

To summarize: There are a lot of things to remember about working with help from outside the library. Here is a Top 10 list:

1. Keep in mind whenever you work with outside help that you are the expert.
2. It is always possible to find inexpensive outside help.
3. Do not assume your library is unimportant just because you do not have a big budget to spend on outside resources.
4. When outside suppliers are working pro bono, do not assume that you are the most important client they have.
5. Do not underestimate the ability of your staff to help with branding work.
6. Let creative people do the creative work.
7. Put your ego aside.
8. Check references.
9. Make sure you clearly define what you expect to be delivered at the end of your project.
10. Have fun! Enjoy the luxury of having outside support and see what you can learn from your consultant as part of the process.

Exercise

Objective

To provide the individual charged with developing a brand additional learning about how to work most effectively with outside help.

Activity

Most librarians are well-connected with fellow librarians. It is a collegial profession in which we all try to learn from each other. Identify five fellow librarians that you feel comfortable chatting with on an informal basis. If you do not have a ready network, call five directors at five libraries near you. (I have yet to find a fellow librarian that will not help if asked.) When you call, ask if you could spend a few minutes picking their brains about any work they might have done with consultants or other outside help. Here are a few questions to ask to get you going:

1. What did you do as part of your project that made your relationship with the outside help either good or bad?
2. How would you manage such a project differently, knowing what you know today?
3. What do you think is the biggest pitfall that a librarian might face when working with outside help? If I ran into that problem, how would you suggest I manage it?
4. Can you suggest anyone else for me to talk with that has managed a project like mine?

As you chat, jot down any good ideas that others might have based on their experience in working with outside help.

-10- Evaluating Your Brand
Short-Term and Long-Term

I t is important that you continuously evaluate your branding plan as you implement it in your library. There will be people involved that will be skeptical about why the library is engaged in branding. They will see it as a commercial activity and not understand why a public/nonprofit entity like a library would need to do it. The more evaluation you do of your branding, the better you will understand if it is working and be able to pass that information on to those who are not vested in the process. There is nothing more convincing than the open sharing of data and information.

The simplest way of evaluating the success of your branding in the short term is to determine how much your board, your staff, and your community are aware of the library and its message *before* you start your branding effort and to follow up by seeing if there is increased awareness as your library starts implementing a branding program. The underlying assumption is that if awareness about your brand increases, there is likely to be a corresponding increase in use of the library. If you already have a brand in place, your goal is first to understand existing levels of awareness about the library brand and then to identify if awareness increases with improved branding practices. Obviously people closely tied to the library are aware of its existence, but they might not have a good idea of what the library's message is (if the library has a message). Give them a quick survey to find out. Then, after you have finished revising your brand and have had it in place for a period of time (no less than three months), give them another survey. You can hope that there will be a big difference!

Below are some basic questions to help you understand current awareness levels among staff, board members, and key library decision makers. This survey should be fielded three to six months before any branding changes and three to six months after such changes, with the objective of seeing increased scores in the second survey. The surveys can be presented

---

? Frequently Asked Question

How do I know when my brand is working?

You will know your brand is working when people are able to tell you what your brand story is. For example, if you say, "Good to the last drop" to someone, she will invariably respond, "Maxwell House Coffee." To get that kind of feedback you need to create a simple, meaningful message that people can mentally file away and pull out when they need it.

---

on paper or online. In the list below each question is followed by a brief explanation of the information it will yield. End each survey with several demographic questions to gain an overview of the respondents (assuming that surveys are submitted anonymously).

1. What do you think is the library's role in the community today? (Depending on the nature of your library, you may need to clarify your intended meaning of *community*. For example, you might say "in the academic community" or "in the college community.") *This is an open-ended question, meaning that respondents have to answer in their own words. The answers will help you understand if your key decision makers understand the library's brand message and if there is consistency in how that message is perceived.*

2. On a scale of 1 to 5 (1 = totally dislike the role, 5 = totally like the role), please rate how much you like this role and think it makes sense for the library. *The answers to this question and question 4 will give you a quantified way to evaluate pre- and post-awareness and approval of the library brand.*

3. Do you think the library's role in the community is the right one? Would you identify a different role for the library? *The responses to these open-ended questions will help you understand if the perceived message of the library is seen as honest.*

4. On a scale of 1 to 5 (1 = totally irrelevant, 5 = totally relevant), please tell us to what extent the library's role in the community is meaningful to you. *The answers to this question and question 2 will give you a quantified way to evaluate pre- and post-awareness and approval of the library brand.*

5. On a scale of 1 to 5 (1 = I cannot remember anything, 5 = I can remember what it looks like, the colors used, all details), please tell us the degree to which you can remember the library's logo. Then please follow up with the details of what you can remember. *You are giving your respondents no clues here about what the library logo looks like so the answers to this question should give you a quantified response as well as details to support that quantification.*

6. What is the library's tagline? *The number of respondents who get the tagline right before versus after branding work will help you understand pre- and post-awareness of the changes in the library brand.*

When you need to measure the response of your community to branding, the process is much the same. You can do a community survey relatively easily by linking to an Internet survey site such as SurveyMonkey.com. This is a good way for nonusers of the library to participate. If you are trying to get high participation levels, you might consider offering an incentive to participation, such as entering all survey respondents (who are interested) in a raffle for a gift certificate. Some nonprofits are uncomfortable with offering incentives because they feel it means they are bribing people for participation and that somehow that will change the survey results. My feeling is that anything that increases participation is a positive and that the results are not so finely tuned that they will be dramatically swayed in any way by a raffle.

If you do not have a library brand at all, you still should do pre- and post-surveys. The results might show that your library has developed a strong awareness in your community over the years simply by doing the same thing consistently and with excellence. You might not have articulated your brand message consciously, but you might have done such a good job of living your message that all of your library users get it without your ever explicitly spelling out what "it" is. In that case you probably want to uncover the brand message that people already sense and start to intentionally articulate it. This is an enviable position to be in because your users already understand what you are about. Now you just have to start telling that story to new users.

It is also possible to evaluate your branding work through subjective analysis. When you do subjective research you ask people to tell you their thoughts about something, but you do not try to quantify their answers. Instead, you listen to what they tell you and try to extrapolate key learning from it. Focus groups are probably the simplest way of gathering subjective research. You might post a sign-up sheet asking users to participate in a short question-and-answer session that will be designed to gather information for the library. If you have trouble getting participants, offer some small incentive, such as a gift certificate to a local bookstore or a free pizza dinner. I would suggest that you tape the session. This will help you later as you review and assess the answers.

You can try several different ways of gathering information in the group. One approach is simply to ask open-ended questions about your branding work and see where the responses take you. For example, you might ask the following questions:

- Can you describe the library's logo?
- Is there anything in particular that you think makes the library unique or special?
- Does the library's logo reflect the thing that makes it unique? If so, how?
- How would you develop a logo for the library?

You can also structure a focus group around a show-and-tell presentation or display examples of current and proposed library logos and ask the participants how they feel about what they are looking at. This type of discussion can be very helpful (and I actually prefer it to the first option of asking open-ended questions) because when you give participants something very specific to respond to, they tend to provide lots of feedback. If you want to both ask open-ended questions and provide examples for participants to respond to, make sure you ask the open-ended questions first. Otherwise, you may find it difficult to move the conversation from the specific to the more general.

All of the suggested analysis will help you understand the extent to which branding is increasing awareness about your library and its programs. If possible, you should also try to gather circulation and traffic statistics both pre-branding and post-branding. If you correlate those numbers with your user input, you will obtain a good idea of whether your brand is building awareness and whether your library is experiencing a corresponding increase in usage. Be prepared to collect data over a long time period to understand the real impact of branding on your library.

Once you have a brand established and regularly include it as a component of your library marketing, you will want to do yearly checkups to make sure your brand continues on target. You can do these checkups in the following ways:

1. Hold a small focus group with several regular library users. Ask them what they think of your brand. Is the brand message still relevant and meaningful to library users? Does the logo look dated, or is it still appropriate for the times? Can users articulate your brand message? Feedback from your loyal users can be very honest and will help you understand if you need to do any brand updating.

2. Communicate with your users via a survey that asks the same questions you would or did use in a focus group. The advantage of a survey is that it enables you to reach a broader audience. I have found that the best way to get a strong response in a public or special library is to put the survey at the circulation desk and ask the staff to mention it to all users over a specific period of time.

Whenever you check up on your branding, make sure that you use at least one quantified question. For example, you might ask the respondents to tell you on a scale of 1 to 5 (1 being poor, 5 being excellent) the degree to which they understand the library's story or think the library's story has meaning to them, or how easy it is for them to remember the library's brand. The question will be determined by what you are trying to do. However, you should ask the same question every year. This will give you a quantified way of measuring from year to year how your brand is doing. Over time you can start to see if the message is becoming less relevant or if people are not remembering the brand.

■ ■ ■ ■

To summarize: It is very important to measure the progress of your branding initiatives. There will be people who do not understand why branding is important, and you will find it very helpful to provide them with data that support the positive results of your work. You can collect data through surveys that are primarily quantitative in nature. You can also collect more subjective input via focus groups. Both methods are useful, particularly when their findings are correlated with statistics related to general library use, such as circulation.

Exercise

Objective

To help the branding project manager understand how to develop an effective survey to gauge response to branding work.

Activity

1. Do an Internet search of *library* and *survey.* You are trying to find two or three miscellaneous library surveys online. It does not really matter what the surveys are about. You will be using them to understand the difference between good and bad survey instruments, not for their subject matter.

2. Once you find your surveys, print hard copies of them. Then take the time to sit down and fill out the surveys. As you are doing this, answer the following questions about each survey question:

    a. Do I understand exactly what this question is asking? (Yes or no) If no, why not?

       b.   Is the author of the question trying to lead me to a specific answer?

       c.   How would a library use this information? (Jot down your thoughts about this.)

3.   Review the survey questions and your responses to questions 2a through 2c above. There are no right or wrong answers.

What you are trying to understand in step 2 is how carefully you need to write your questions to ensure that they are clear and do not bias respondents' answers. I wrote a survey at one point in which I asked, "Why do you think the library is a special place?" Eight hundred fifty people responded without complaint. The 851st respondent told me that he was insulted that I had assumed that the library was a special place and that by doing so I had biased the survey. The hardest part of accepting his response was that he was correct. By evaluating other people's surveys you should start to understand how you will need to write your own.

Your answers to question 2c are especially important. You should never ask a question in a survey because it would be nice to know the answer. Whenever I sense a question I have written is moving in that direction, I ask myself, "OK, if I get this information, so what? Who will care?" This helps me ensure that I am not wasting my time or my respondents' time. I also always challenge myself to know what action the answer to a specific question will provoke. For example, if I ask respondents to use a scale of 1 to 5 to rate how much they like a logo and their answers average out to 4, I know I do not need to make any more design changes to my logo. If the average of the scores is 2, then I know I need to continue making changes until I hit an average of 4 or higher. It is crucial to keep your survey or focus group meeting as short and to-the-point as possible so that you collect only the information that is directly relevant to your project.

■11■ Maintaining Your Brand

You have developed the perfect library message and a great tagline to tell your library users your story. You hired a good designer who created the ideal logo for your library. You made a smart staff member the brand advocate, and you have been measuring your results. Your users are telling you that they understand your story and know what the library is about, and there is strong awareness of the library in your community. You have done it all! Now the question is, how do you keep doing it? How do you keep your brand honest, and how do you keep your library in your users' thought processes?

The Brand Training Program

Begin by thinking about how you can make sure your brand permeates every aspect of your library. You want everyone on your staff saying the same thing when it comes to the brand message, and you want everyone on the staff using the brand identity in the same way. If your staff has worked on the branding project, then training them will not be very difficult. They will already know the why's of branding and just need very clear direction about the how's.

If possible, have one training session for the entire staff. This ensures that everyone hears the same thing at the same time, and it will give staff a chance to ask questions of both the branding project manager and each other. I would cover four things at the training session. First, review the editorial standards for the brand. Give everyone a chance to ask questions. Second, review the design standards. Again, give everyone a chance to ask questions. Third, discuss the role of the brand advocate and talk about who will be doing that work. Make sure everyone knows that they can always go to the brand advocate with questions. Fourth and finally, if your library has developed templates for promotional materials, train the staff in how those templates can and should be used. If possible, set up computers to allow staff to experiment with the templates and see how they work.

At the end of the training session, the project manager should talk about the key factor in the success of branding: the staff. To make branding successful on an ongoing basis staff members need to become brand ambassadors or advocates or promoters (all terms used in the branding literature of today). A brand ambassador is anyone who is passionate about the brand, is willing to talk about it, and may even volunteer brand information on her own. I am sure everyone reading this book knows at least one brand ambassador. Think about a friend or family member who has found a product or service he loves and talks about it all the time. Such people will laud their product (think about the first generation of iPod users) and tell you all the wonderful things they have found about it. Some well-known brand ambassadors are Saturn car buyers, people who ride Harley motorcycles, women who own Coach purses, and people who find a great, honest car repair shop. You get the idea. A brand ambassador for the library is anyone who is willing to talk about the library, loves the library, and spreads the word about the library.

Most librarians could name three or four library users right off the bat who are natural ambassadors. What those librarians never consider is that they too probably fall into that category. Librarians tend to be somewhat quiet about their skills, and they are absolutely the last people in the world to toot their own horns. Most of them would be very uncomfortable with the idea of extolling their own virtues. But how about if they were to extol the virtues of the library as a community gathering place or praise the library's collection? These are things they understand and can speak about knowledgeably—and they are not being immodest in doing so. If all staff members who see themselves as ambassadors were to talk with all their inherent passion about the library, the library would immediately gain a whole new cadre of supporters in the community. Most people decide if they are willing to try something based on the recommendation of a friend or neighbor. If twenty library employees each tell twenty friends who tell twenty friends about all the wonderful things available at the library, then there are four hundred people who are more likely to walk in your library's doors! If each of those four hundred tells another twenty, . . . you start to build a whole new group of people to support the library.

So, when you are training staff about branding, at the very end, do not be afraid to ask them to become brand ambassadors. Talk about what being an ambassador means and explain the benefit to them (a library that is well supported and well funded). Ask them for ideas about how they might become brand emissaries. (Some libraries print up buttons for staff members to wear at work that say, "Ask me about the library!") My guess is that you will be able to get at least half of your staff on board, and that is a good start.

Once staff has been trained, I would recommend similar training for members of the board or other decision-making body for the library. This training can be shorter than that for staff. Essentially, I would focus on why branding is important and then talk about some of the ways in which branding will be implemented at the library. At this point the board will have been in the loop for the branding process and will understand why the work is being done, so you should not be telling them anything new or concerning. Rather, this training is meant to update them and fill in any gaps they might have in their understanding of branding. Make a point of asking all board members to become active brand ambassadors. Board members are much more effective if they are willing to tell others in the community why they are passionate about the library. You might consider putting together a presentation for board members titled "Why I'm a Library Ambassador" that they can present to different groups in your community. If you can get board and staff members to tell others why they support the library, you will have gone a long way toward ensuring the long-term success of your branding.

Something that needs to be clear to all staff and board members is that *all* patron experiences must support the brand concept. This means from the minute people walk in the door of your library, they should be experiencing the library brand. Assume that your brand message is that the library is "Where the community connects." When a patron walks in the door, she should be greeted cheerfully by library staff at the circulation or reference desk. It would make sense to have a prominent location for a community bulletin board. If there are regular community events at the library, information about them should be readily apparent when someone walks in the door. Because *connects* could also apply to computer connections, it would make sense to have more than enough computers to allow users quick access. Librarians would need to understand the community in which they work and be able to share that information with their users. Bottom line, the library should consider all the different ways in which it could epitomize its message and then deliver on those ways at the highest level possible.

Evaluating the Brand

The library can ensure that its brand continues to be relevant by evaluating on a regular basis (at least yearly) the extent to which it is meeting its users' needs, not just in terms of tasks accomplished but also in the emotional realm. A task to be accomplished might be something like fulfilling 95 percent of interlibrary loans or increasing circulation every year by 5 percent or having more participants this year than last year in a summer reading program. Most libraries already collect statistics to evaluate the extent to which they are meeting such users' needs. Meeting emotional needs is an entirely different concept. Emotional needs might be something like "It feels friendly and welcoming when I walk in the door" or "Staff always seem happy to talk with me" or "I always leave feeling that I have connected with other people in my community."

Measuring your organization's ability to meet users' emotional needs requires a bit of ingenuity. One approach is to recruit some of your regular users to become the equivalent of secret shoppers. Give each person a list of the qualities you are hoping your library delivers, for instance, "friendly," "feels welcoming," and so forth. Also give each secret shopper an evaluation form to fill out during his next library visit. On the form, you might divide the library experience into specific activities, such as entering the library, talking to reference, asking questions at administration, or checking out books. The objective is to identify areas where specific emotional needs are not being met and to figure out solutions.

Another approach is to ask staff members to do their own assessment of the degree to which specific emotional needs are being met in the library. One morning, before users arrive, invite selected staff members to walk through and evaluate the library for attributes such as "welcoming," "cozy," "friendly"—whatever traits your library seeks to project. If the library's space does not score well on certain attributes, ask staff members what they would change to improve the situation and make the library more reflective of its desired brand personality.

Building Relationships with Users

Another way to maintain your brand year after year is to build ongoing relationships with your library users. This requires that you communicate with your users more than once or twice a year via a survey. Try to find ways in which they can give you feedback on a regular basis. A library Board of Trustees is an example of a group of users who provide regular feedback to the library. However, that feedback tends to address administration and management rather than the day-to-day running of the library. The key to building ongoing relationships with users is to establish opportunities for two-way communication.

Blogs

Blogs are an amazing tool for libraries. They can take the place of the old comments box that most libraries had. What makes blogs incredibly powerful (and a bit scary) is that they enable a library user to have a quick dialogue with librarians or administrators, and the results can be shared with the community as a whole. Thus, the management of the library tends to become very transparent, which in turn makes more people feel that they have a voice in the running of the library.

Advisory Groups

Many libraries have teen advisory groups. Why not have an adult advisory group? Or, in the case of my community, which has many retirees, how about a seniors advisory group? Or, if your library is trying to meet the needs of a new immigrant community, how about a newcomers advisory group? One of the best ways of improving your relationship with your community is by reaching out to individuals and groups who understand its needs. Develop a group of individuals to whom you can go for information and advice about community issues affecting the library.

Appealing to Specific Interests

Find board members with special passions and then ask them how the library might better serve the needs of individuals with similar concerns. At my library we have one board member who is a new mom. She finds that visiting the library is an invaluable way of getting out of the house and keeping in touch with other moms who are facing the same issues she is dealing with. She and I are talking about how we might tap into this group to get more information about how the library can better serve them.

A library, like any other branded product, needs constant tending to grow and be effective. The ideas presented in this chapter should prove to be helpful in this enterprise.

■ ■ ■ ■

To summarize: Much like a car, a brand requires regular maintenance to keep it running efficiently and effectively. Training library staff and board members to become brand ambassadors is one way to keep your library brand alive and vibrant in your community. Evaluating your message to ensure that it stays fresh and relevant is another. Finally, by developing two-way communication with brand users, you can keep in touch with how your patrons are viewing your brand and what changes might need to be made.

Exercise

Objective

To drive home to your Core Team that being a brand ambassador can be as simple as being thoughtful about opportunities for discussing the library.

Activity

After you have gone through the branding process (brand audit, developing a brand story and visual support, writing brand standards and putting in place a brand advocate), ask your Core Team to take the following quiz:

1. State the library's story in one sentence.
2. Write down the single most important thing to you about this library.
3. Estimate the number of people to whom you have mentioned the library over the past week.

Then ask the Core Team members to read their answers aloud. In all likelihood everyone will be able to respond to item 1 with no issue, and most will probably be able to tell you a good answer to item 2. However, item 3 frequently stops people dead in their tracks. Your Core Team needs to remember that the library is only as good as the number of people who are aware of it and use it. Ask team members to keep the library in the front of their minds as they go through the week and to bring the library into their conversation each time an appropriate opportunity arises. To follow up, ask them to e-mail you at the end of the week to report how many people they discussed the library with *that* week, and share those e-mails with all members of the Core Team. The idea is to demonstrate to your Core Team that their awareness of opportunities to advocate for the library and their willingness to do so can significantly increase community awareness.

■12■ Blogs and Brands

Marketing is based around the concept of telling a story about your brand to consumers. The objective is to give them enough information so that they understand why your product or service is the best one for them to buy or use. Consumers listen to advertising as a way of collecting information about a brand. However, family and friends have always been an even more convincing source of details about products and services that are being considered for purchase.

Today, the Internet has vastly expanded the amount of information available about products and services. New forms of advertising have been developed just for the Internet. The circle of family and friends has grown to encompass the virtual world. In this environment it has become very difficult for suppliers to say anything about their products or services that a consumer cannot easily research for veracity.

Initially, organizations were afraid of Internet conversations about their products and services. They were concerned that they would be put in a bad light, that incorrect information would be circulated in the marketplace, or that they would be called to account if their products did not function optimally. However, organizations gradually realized that there was value in these consumer-to-consumer discussions. Companies could ask questions, they could ask for feedback about potential products or services, and they could address questions and issues from potential users. The really progressive organizations started asking for help from their customers and potential customers to develop new products and services. They stopped being afraid of consumers' online conversations and instead started using them as a source of inspiration and development for their brands.

The moral of the story is simple: the Internet offers libraries an opportunity to start having more *conversations* with their users and to incorporate the resulting feedback into building improved products and services. I have frequently seen examples of libraries *telling* users what services the library provides without ever considering if those services are useful or meaningful to the intended recipients. Today consumers can get almost any information they want about a product or service on their own. They do not need a mere list of what services are available; that information is relatively easy to come by. Instead, of much more value to consumers is information about *why* your products are unique or special or particularly worthy of their time and interest.

When libraries develop more of a dialogue with their patrons, they increase their opportunities to get feedback about issues with which they have been struggling. For example, public libraries frequently bemoan the public's lack of awareness and use of databases as tools of research. I see two potential reasons why consumers have not jumped at the availability of databases. First, it could be that libraries have not done a good job of telling consumers about databases or have not shared a story about why databases could be helpful, both of which are marketing issues. Second, it might be that libraries told consumers a good story but did not stop to ask their listeners whether or not they care about databases—and maybe they do not. (I know, this is heresy of the highest order!) The point is that we need to do more listening to what our consumers want and stop trying to tell them what they need. When we do listen we also have to understand that our library users cannot always tell us what they want. Sometimes they can only describe the problem they are facing and hope that we might have a solution.

Enter blogs. A blog is a user-generated website where writers put their thoughts down and readers can respond. To an older generation it would be much like putting a diary in a public place where readers could add their own thoughts and comments after reading the entries. *Blog* actually stands for *web log*. Blogs might be one of the best tools library marketers can put into place—if they are brave enough to do so and willing to work at the process. It can be daunting to put a tool into place that will give people the chance to tell you what you are doing wrong. The worst part is that you are putting that tool right out there on the town square where anyone can read it! I admit that I myself find this intimidating. However, when you know what people are saying, you can address it, thus avoiding the possibility that it will unexpectedly pop up during budget season. If I am planning to go to my town government to ask for the addition of a new position in my budget, it would be very helpful if I could produce feedback from a library blog that says, "We want a librarian who can do X, Y, and Z."

I bring up the subject of blogs in conjunction with branding because I think blogs can be one of the best ways to get regular feedback about your library brand. You can ask questions on a blog. People can tell you if they like your library story. They can tell you if they think your brand story is honest. They can even tell you how they feel about your logo. You can use a blog to talk about the new products and services at your library. You can use a blog to describe a possible database purchase and ask for feedback about its usefulness or desirability. You can use blogs to promote special events. Basically, blogs can become your own personal form of conversation with your patrons.

Of course, the difficulty with a blog is that once you ask for input, look out. You will get it, and you need to be prepared to deal with it. A blog can become either an indispensable or a hated part of a library director's life. Questions have to be answered, problems addressed, and ideas considered. Once a blog is let loose it can become a destructive force if you fail to pay attention to it. If you lack the time necessary to maintain a blog, you will do your brand a major disservice (remember the importance of brand honesty?), so it is better to leave blogging to other libraries.

The good news is that a blog essentially provides something that most libraries have been providing for years—a comments box for users. A comments box always felt safer, however, because you could deal with issues in private and did not have to expose them to the whole community. Then again, if an issue does become public, someone might come up with a great idea about how to address it. Or people might be happy to participate in the conversation and feel even more connected to the library. Or you can use a blog as a wonderful way of gaining insight into your library brand, how people respond to it, what aspects of the brand are working, and what needs to change. If you ask people what they think, it is amazing what they will tell you. You just need to figure out how you will respond to keep the lines of communication open.

Before you start a blog about your new library brand, consider your level of risk tolerance. You have to be willing to be very open about what is happening at your library, and you need to make sure your board (and staff) is equally willing to be that open. You should set some parameters before you start the blog, including topics that will not be discussed, such as personnel or political issues. You also need to develop an internal process for responding to the blog: Who will respond? Over what time periods? When would the board or library decision makers get involved? Setting parameters will not limit the conversation, but it will help keep the conversation focused on the areas in which you are interested.

No matter what limits you set, do not be too surprised if writers in your brand blog go off your desired topic. Someone might start talking about service at your circulation desk when you have asked about a new program. Someone might write about a program that she just attended when you have asked about new budget ideas. The key with a blog is not to get too absorbed in your agenda. Try to follow your library users where they lead you. In the midst of all the complaints about parking that you have heard a million times before you will find new ideas, different perspectives, and unconventional approaches that will open your eyes and give you some new directions to consider.

You should also think about how you will manage the information you receive. You might spend ten minutes during weekly or biweekly staff meetings discussing input and responses. You might funnel ideas or comments to department heads. You might ask staff members to manage the blog and to send the questions and comments to appropriate people in the library. However you decide to manage the blog, make sure that your entire staff understands what you are doing and why. People will find it very threatening to read unpleasant comments about their work. What you need to reinforce is that the blog is a tool for improving the library's work, not a method of punishment for hard-working librarians. Above·all, do not request feedback and then ignore it—that would be massively disrespectful of the people who took the time to contribute to the blog.

If you can develop a blog that is read regularly by a core group of users, it can become a valuable tool for the library. It can become an advisory group, giving you input about topics far beyond your brand. It can be used as a source of information or to rally support during budget season. In many ways, a blog can help you do more listening to your users.

You can implement a blog simply by signing up for an account at any one of the many free services available on the Internet. Or you can have a web designer develop a blog just for your library's website. You might also consider asking your patrons to help you develop a blog for the library. This truly enters into the spirit of blogging, which is basically "Let the users help develop the product."

After you have figured out how to put a blog in place, do not forget to identify how you will market your blog. Some libraries put a blog on their website and then just quietly wait for users to discover its existence. Some-

Tip

Keep all blogs fresh. Put up a topic for discussion, give it a week, and then move on to the next topic if you do not get much response. People return only to blogs that are refreshed on a regular basis. Because your goal is customer input, keep your topics updated and interesting.

times people find the blog; sometimes they do not. It is usually more effective to actively market your blog. Make sure your staff understands how to use the blog themselves. Then you could consider offering training sessions on the blog to your library users. You should probably put out brochures explaining how the blog works, and you will want to put similar material on your website itself. I would also suggest putting out a news release about the library's development of its own blog. Talk about why the library has a blog, how the library would like to get users involved, and where users can go to get more information about the blog. Also, do not forget to share information about the blog with library decision makers, such as your board or administration. These individuals should be good advocates for the library, and this is a good opportunity to enlist their help in spreading the word. As your marketing plan is executed, do not be surprised to see a large increase in readership of your blog that will then diminish over time. That is OK, you will retain the readers who are truly interested and involved in the library.

Today there are a million blogs out in cyberspace. Before you implement your own blog, check out some that already exist. You can Google the word *blog* and a topic of interest. For example, you might type in "blog dogs" or "blog dog training Maine." Read some of the blogs that come up and decide what you like and do not like about them. Then see if some of those ideas will help as you develop your own blog. A blog can be as simple as a conversation between two friends or as complicated as a presentation to the United Nations. You need to determine what will work for your library and brand.

One caveat: work very hard at keeping your blog free of jargon. Reliance on jargon seems to be one of the universal traps that writers fall into without realizing it. (I may well be doing it right now.) Jargon is the writer's way of guarding her own private universe; it ensures that only people who speak the same language will be allowed in. The whole point of a branding blog is to invite in people of all different backgrounds and perspectives so that you can gain a real understanding of what the world thinks about your library. One way to avoid the jargon trap is to ask a friend or family member who is not a librarian to read some of your blog entries before you post them. That person will ask you simple questions like "What does ILL mean?" that should help wake you up when you are using jargon. Then over time you will start to develop your own internal monitor. The more open, accessible, and jargon-free you can make your blog, the more useful it will be in helping you improve your branding process.

Always be forthright in your blog. If you have an opinion (versus a fact) that you want to express, go ahead and do that. However, do not forget to tell people your agenda. Bloggers tend to respond harshly to dishonesty, so my suggestion is to always challenge yourself to be as forthright as possible.

■ ■ ■ ■

To summarize: Blogs can be a particularly effective tool for brand advocates to use to encourage users to share their thoughts about the library. Before starting a blog a library should identify how it will manage the information it receives through the blog, who will be involved in running the blog, and how the blog will be marketed to the community.

Exercise

Objective

To demonstrate to the Core Team how libraries are using blogs to learn about and better serve their users.

Activity

Go to the Ann Arbor District Library website (www.aadl.org). The Ann Arbor library has put blogs to use in many different ways on its website, and its approach provides some good food for thought about how another library might do the same. Consider in particular how the following blogs reflect the library's willingness to open itself to feedback:

- The director's blog
- The book review blogs
- Feedback from the community blogs

Have the Core Team review the Ann Arbor library's website and discuss how the same types of blogs might be employed to gain a better understanding of your library's brand and how your library's users are responding to that brand. Ask the team members what their concerns might be about developing a blog. Start to identify some of the features that you want to include in your blog. Then start a very simple blog that is available only to the members of your Core Team. Ask them to use the blog for a week to understand its pros and cons.

▪13▪ Common Pitfalls and False Assumptions

I have talked a great deal in this book about how to build a library brand. I want to make it clear that I see branding as a very possible project for any library, regardless of level of expertise. To that end, I have tried to be very positive about how simple branding work can be. However, I think it is also important to understand where the potential pitfalls can be found. I thought I would take this opportunity to talk about surefire ways to ensure that your library brand will be a failure. The goal of this chapter is not to discourage libraries from developing brands but rather to point out some of the potential obstacles to successful branding. Consider this as a test at the end of this book. If you already know that all the points below are don'ts, you have assimilated the basics of this book and are well on your way to developing a successful library brand.

1. *Exclude your staff from the branding process.* This is probably the first and best way to ensure failure. Frequently librarians are not included in marketing or branding activities because they are assumed to lack the requisite skills. However, what librarians cannot bring to the table in terms of branding experience they can more than compensate for in terms of intelligence and understanding of their organization. Librarians are on the front lines every day. They know their users, they know their collection, and they know the community in which they work. If anyone has a sense of what makes a library important in a community, it is the librarians who work there. Plus, if you do not involve them in the work of developing a brand, what personal involvement or commitment will they have in making the brand work? Librarians have lots of other work to do, so if they do not see branding as important, you can rest assured that a branding program will not be implemented. Consequently, you exclude your staff at your own peril. If you do

include them, you can be certain that they will bring tremendous value to the process. Librarians are smart folk!

2. *Fail to set clear expectations with your decision-making body about what branding can and cannot do.* Because branding is so new to most libraries, most people do not understand what branding can and cannot do for an organization. They may assume that branding will be the ultimate marketing tool that will solve all of their awareness issues. Or they may think that branding is a nice little side project that really is not all that important. Bottom line, branding is neither. Like most projects, it will deliver in proportion to what is put into it. It is important for a branding project manager to define exactly what branding will do for an organization. Branding will help an organization develop a clear message about what makes it unique and meaningful in the life of a potential user. Branding will help an organization focus its activities around the delivery of the attributes defined by its message. Branding will not be a cure-all because it is only one element in the marketing mix. The most effective marketing project will make branding its first step: a message must be developed before it can be delivered. By the same token, it is crucial to remember that branding is the first step, not the only step, in the process of communicating with users.

3. *Do not do your homework before starting.* A branding project is much more likely to be successful if the branding project manager starts by reading books on branding, looking at how other libraries have done branding, and spending time thinking about what branding is. That is why this book has so many exercises: the more you work through the basics of branding, the more likely you are to acquire the instinctive know-how you need to succeed at branding your library. I have found that it is helpful to collect examples of branding that I do not like and that do not seem effective and then try to figure out what prompted my negative reaction. Doing the same will help you start to build your own set of criteria for what works and what does not work. If a project manager jumps into branding unprepared, the really important elements of branding (like defining the brand message) will most likely get overlooked because the manager will not understand how such work can contribute to the overall process. In contrast, if you have thought about branding, looked at other libraries' brands, and considered which brands do and do not work for you, you are much more likely to start your branding project with some degree of understanding and conviction. That will result in a stronger end product for you.

4. *If you do not have a budget, do not even start branding. It is too hard to do it all yourself.* Unfortunately, I think a lot of libraries get stuck in this thought process. Because branding is new, many librarians are intimidated by it and

are afraid to try it without an expert helping them. I hope that a key message you got out of this book is that branding is common sense, not brain surgery. If you do some self-training, you can do a good portion of it on your own. For the things that are harder to do on your own (such as design), you can usually find someone to help you for little or no cost if you are creative in your searching. In fact, I always tell people to keep in mind that branding is actually a lot of fun. It is a combination of psychology, creativity, and gut instinct. In the marketing industry, almost everyone likes to do branding because it is enjoyable, interesting, and subjective, meaning there is no definitive right or wrong. It does not require working with a lot of numbers and data. Rather, it involves creativity and the willingness to try to think the way your users do. Approach branding as something that will bring a lot of energy and enthusiasm to your library, not as an uncomfortable job that you got stuck with. Adopting a positive attitude is the first way to have a lot more fun.

5. *Tell your community that you are developing a library brand but do not tell them why.* Unfortunately, people that do not understand branding see it as a dirty word that implies either exploitation (which this book should have convinced you is false) or that the library called in outside experts and paid them a lot of taxpayer or tuition money. My suggestion for avoiding both of these problems is to make sure that whenever you talk about the branding work your library is doing, you also talk about *why* you are doing it. Make sure your audience understands that branding is about developing a message and conveying information; it is not about forcing people to buy a product or service that they do not want. It also helps if you articulate who is doing the work and how you got them involved. Most libraries have volunteers participating in their branding process. If you can talk about your volunteer branding team, it will become clear to all that you have not spent large sums of money to hire expensive consultants. And, as a bonus, the combination of staff involvement and community participation in the branding project makes a good public relations story.

6. *Develop a logo for the library but do not do anything else because a logo is all that is important.* By this point in this book you completely understand why this is not true. A logo is important because it is the visual representation of your organization and should help you tell your library's story. However, unless you have done a very good job of conveying your story through your library's work, it is important to have a logo and a message or tagline combined. Part of the power of developing a library message is the amount of thought and collaboration that goes into the process. Many people in the organization have to sit down together and find a common perspective. Then

they have to spend even more time considering how to convey that message to their community. A library that skips such work and just creates a logo loses a wonderful opportunity to build a team and focus the organization's strategic energies.

7. *Do not refer to your library mission or vision when developing a branding message because a mission and a message are very different things.* A library's brand message, vision, and mission are indeed very different things. The library's mission defines what the library is trying to do today. The library's vision conveys its long-term goals for the future. And the brand message is a direct communication to the library's users that tells what the library can do for them. However, even though each of these statements serves a different purpose, if they have no relationship to each other, then there will be some very confusing messages floating around. A library should have a mission, vision, and branding story that all relate to and support each other. If your team is developing a branding message based on your library's mission or vision, then constantly compare the two to make sure they relate to each other. Otherwise, you could easily end up with a library staff going in six different directions, trying to achieve very different ends.

8. *Do not bother writing brand standards because no one will read them anyway.* In the course of developing this book and doing branding and strategic planning at my own library, I have gotten involved in several discussions with library leaders about planning in general. Frequently, the leader's perspective was that no one ever looks at planning after it is done, so there is no point in doing it. My viewpoint is very different. I think planning is extraordinarily important if it is referred to on a regular basis after it is done. Brand standards are a wonderful example of this. If they are created as a living document, people refer to them regularly. If a librarian has a question about how a logo should look in a promotion document, she can go to the brand standards to find out. When a document is used like that in an organization, it tends to become very powerful. So if you go to all the work of developing brand standards, make sure you also get them inculcated into your organization. Train your staff to use the brand standards. Explain how the standards actually empower them because once they know the rules, they can do their work without constantly checking in with authorities for permission. Then, support this stance by letting your library team try out some branding work on their own, checking in with the brand advocate only with questions or specific issues. This approach will make brand standards a very effective tool for your library.

9. *Do all the branding work internally. It will save the library money.* I know I said above that branding is not brain surgery and that anyone can do it. I stand by this statement. However, I also believe that if you have the money to pay for at least a designer, then you should spend that money. I have said before that graphic design is a unique skill and not everyone has it. If you have no other recourse, then you will have to do the designing yourself, and I am sure that you can do a reasonable job. However, if you can find someone to help you, the results will be that much better for your library. To lay the groundwork, make sure you can clearly and succinctly articulate why branding is important for your library. Take your decision-making body through your thought process, making sure that they understand why design work is important and that it is not easy to do for an amateur. You can hope that this will help you gain some sort of budget to do your design work.

10. *Only big city libraries need brands.* Obviously, this is also not true. Because branding requires a clear story about what makes a library special and meaningful in the life of its community, it is useful to libraries of all sizes. A small library frequently needs to justify its budget more than a big city library does. A branding message will help to clarify the value that a library brings to its community and why that value is unique. The usefulness of a strong message about the role the library plays can never be underestimated, regardless of the size of the community.

■ ■ ■ ■

To summarize: Branding can be successfully carried out by using common sense and careful thought. Nonetheless, some pitfalls need to be avoided to facilitate the branding process. Among the most common are excluding your staff from the process; failing to set clear expectations about what branding can and cannot do; failing to do your homework before starting; assuming that branding cannot be done without a big budget; not sharing the reasons for branding with your community; limiting your branding effort to the development of a logo; not basing your branding on your library's mission/vision; failing to write and enforce brand standards; not considering how outside support could contribute to your branding project; and assuming that only big city libraries do branding.

Exercise

Objective

To give your Core Team the opportunity to work through the entire branding process and identify questions or issues that they still might have.

Activity

Give your Core Team a copy of several pages from the website of the Boston Public Library, the New York Public Library, or any well-known library that is already branded. Break your Core Team into groups of two or three people, and tell them that they are responsible for branding the selected library. Ask each group to spend 45 minutes answering the following questions (the teams will need access to the Internet for this exercise):

1. Who do they think should be involved in the process of branding that library? Name categories of people, such as Friends of the Library, board members, and influential community members—not specific individuals.

2. Go to the specified library's website and do a quick brand audit, identifying the extent to which you think the brand has a clear, meaningful message; an attention-grabbing visual identity; consistent usage; and an effort to be honest.

3. Based on your brand audit, define a new brand message (or tell why the existing brand message should be retained), identify how you would change (or why you would keep) the brand's existing visual elements, and what tagline you would write for the redesigned brand.

4. Finally, how would you evaluate the success of your new brand?

Ask each group to briefly report their decisions and results. More important than reviewing each team's answers is discussing questions that came up about the process or how to work through the branding procedure.

Appendix

■ A ■ Case Studies

The case studies in this appendix demonstrate some of the different ways in which branding is being done at libraries. They are based on questions that grew out of my own experience with branding. One of my key objectives was to understand how much background a library had in marketing or branding before it started its branding project. Through this process I discovered two things. First, there are very few libraries that have gone through a branding process. I think the number is so small because libraries are either intimidated by branding or still do not understand what branding can do for them. Second, the libraries that did branding often had very little experience in it but still managed to do a good job because they used common sense and trusted their own intuition about what was right for their organization. Due to the uniqueness of each situation, no library will end up doing branding work in exactly the same way as another library. Each organization has to determine what it wants to achieve from a branding project and how it is going to use the subsequent results.

The libraries in some of the cases provided here did not follow the process laid out in this book. Their approaches are included to demonstrate that it is OK to just go out and get started and that you do not have to be perfect in the process. Even if you do every aspect of a branding project yourself, the results will make a big difference to your organization. Do not be afraid of branding (or marketing), and do not hesitate to experiment to find out what works best for your library.

To see additional figures, including some in color, please see the online version of appendix A at www.ala.org/editions/extras/Doucett09621.

Lucius Beebe Memorial Library
Wakefield, Massachusetts
Sharon Gilley, Director
Liz Doucett, Assistant Director

Description of project

Beebe Library lacked a clearly identified brand message and tagline so the library director and assistant director decided to focus on developing them. At the same time the administrators wanted to revise the existing logo to include the new tagline (figure 4). Because they wanted the new materials to be used throughout the library, they also decided to develop a set of new brand standards (editorial and design), including a revision of the library brand's color palette, standardization of logo use, and standardization of fonts. Finally, because they wanted staff to be able to create marketing materials on their own, they hired a designer to help construct a template that could be used by any staff member in the production of promotional materials. The template was a standardized layout for marketing materials (flyers, bookmarks, posters) that had some features that were fixed and some elements of design (colors, pictures) that could be changed by staff, depending on the event or project being marketed.

Did you see this as a branding project, or did you view it as something else?

This project was seen as a branding project initially and then evolved into a broader marketing project as we decided to develop promotional templates.

Who initiated the project and why?

The author of this book, Elisabeth Doucett, initiated the project because she and the library director, Sharon Gilley, identified the need for a clear message about the library's role in the community. There was a wonderful logo that had been designed when the library was remodeled and updated in 1999. The library director wanted to maintain that logo but also saw the need to formulate a clear brand message and to revise the logo to include the message.

Figure 4
Revised Beebe Library logo with tagline

Who was involved in the project, and what was each person's relationship to the library?

The project was executed by the library's director, assistant director, and staff. An outside graphic designer (Susan Edwards of Extra Mile Design) was brought in to revise the existing logo, write brand standards, and create a marketing template.

Who ran the project?

The assistant director of the library ran the project with regular input from the library director.

What was your objective for the project, and do you think you achieved that objective?

The primary objective of the project was to develop a clear brand message and to integrate it into the existing library logo. The objective was definitely achieved. After hard work on the part of the library staff, a brand message and subsequent tagline were identified. With the help of the outside graphic designer, the existing logo and the new tagline were integrated into a revised logo that is now being used in all library promotional materials.

How did you measure success?

Success was defined as the development of a tagline that could be effectively integrated with our existing logo.

What do you think you did particularly well in this project?

The participation of staff at the very beginning of the project made a big difference in their interest and involvement in the project. The integration of the existing logo with the new tagline was executed well because the team worked hard ahead of time to understand the library's role in the community. The use of an outside graphic designer who understood what we were trying to do in the project made a big difference in the success of the final outcome.

What do you think could have gone better?

The project took longer than anticipated. The work had to be done around all of the other responsibilities that I had as an assistant director. Therefore, it frequently was not my top priority. I think we did not develop a clear measurement of success for the project. In retrospect, I would have been more careful about that because an established indicator of strong success helps you make a case for continuing work of this nature (marketing) in the future. I also thought we should have spent more time training our library board about branding and why it was important. They were supportive but not particularly enthusiastic about the project. If they had been more strongly involved, I think the branding work might have gone further and progressed faster.

Did you get staff involved and, if so, how? If not, why not?

The library staff were involved in every element of this project. They worked on identifying the characteristics that make Beebe Library unique and wrote taglines that articulated that uniqueness. The intention to introduce marketing templates also made it important to include staff in the entire process. They would be responsible for using the templates to develop future promotional materials so it was important for them to accept the templates and learn how to use them. As we went through the branding process, the staff were trained consistently about marketing and branding. We wanted them to share in the ownership of branding and felt we could accomplish that only if the staff really understood what we were trying to do.

Did you develop brand standards as part of this project? If not, how do you maintain consistency in your branding work?

Both editorial and design standards were developed as part of this project. All staff were given copies of both and trained in how to use them. We hope that over time this approach will provide the consistency needed to ensure the brand look is maintained. When staff members came to me with questions I would refer them to the brand standards so that they would get used to using those as their guidelines. My ultimate objective was to make everyone an owner of the branding process.

What advice do you have for a library initiating a branding project?

Make sure you have someone involved in the project who is excited by it and is willing to champion it. Branding takes time and energy, and it is hard to incorporate into an organization if there is no one leading the charge. The person running a branding project does not have to be an expert in the topic. However, he does have to have a real interest in learning and be willing to talk about what he is learning so that he can energize other staff members to get involved.

Make sure your director is on board. Before we started branding, my director and I had many conversations to make sure that she understood and supported what I wanted to do. As a result, once we started the process she was more than willing to participate in it and work to rally the support it needed.

If possible, persuade your library to provide enough money for you to hire a professional graphic designer. As I say many times in this book, you can do a very good job of branding without the help of a professional designer. However, once you work with one, you start to really understand the value they bring to the process. They have a unique, artistic eye and thought process that really makes the difference between good and outstanding.

Develop a timetable, work it out carefully—and then add a month to it. I found that no matter how hard I tried to keep to our timetable, something would invariably slip. In a corporation a project tends to keep moving forward because everyone has the same agenda. In a nonprofit organization it is much harder to make things happen by specific dates because so many people are involved in the process and all are trying to do many different jobs. Accept that things will take longer than you want and you can avoid burning yourself out.

Ipswich Public Library
Ipswich, Massachusetts
Victor Dyer, Director
Genevieve Picard, Assistant Director

Description of project

The library director, Victor Dyer, felt that the Ipswich Public Library needed a new logo to represent the new, exciting activities going on at the library. The library had just completed an addition, and he believed the time was right for branding.

As the director considered this idea, he spent a lot of time studying the library, looking for inspiration for a logo. One day he noticed the beautiful grillwork in the older part of the building and realized that it was exactly what he was looking for. The grillwork became the focal point of design efforts and eventually led to the final logo for the library (figure 5).

The director asked Ed Emberley, a resident of Ipswich and a Caldecott Award winner, to play with the idea of a design. Emberley came up with several variations, including one for the children's room (figure 6), and they decided to go with that option. The logo won an award from the Massachusetts Library Association in 2001.

Figure 5 Ipswich Public Library logo on brochure

The library began using the new logo on its stationery, library cards, website, and newsletter; to promote a one book program; as a banner for a special program for children; and on the cover of the library's plan of service. Today the logo is used in a newspaper column and on all of the library's brochures. For fun, the library even made play eyeglasses for kids using the children's logo.

Figure 6 Ipswich Public Library logo for youth services

*Did you see this as a branding project or did you
view it as something else?*

The project was always meant to develop a logo for the library.

Who initiated the project and why?

The library director initiated the project. He shared the work done on the logo with the library trustees, and they voted to accept the logo as official. During that process the director showed the trustees all of the many ways in which the logo could be used, and that helped convince them of its appropriateness. A key objective of the project was to develop a logo that would have flexibility and that could be used in many different ways, depending on the needs of the library.

Initially the library was fairly conservative about how it used the logo, putting it on such traditional items as business cards and stationery. Then, as administrators and staff became more comfortable with the concept, they started to play with the logo. As an example, initially the logo was used in one way on the library business card. Then the logo was blown up larger and bled out to the edge of the business card with more distinctive colors. Over time the library has found more and more ways in which it can evolve the logo.

*Who was involved in the project, and what was
each person's relationship to the library?*

The library director started the project. The actual logo design was done by illustrator Ed Emberley. The library director was assisted by the library's assistant director, Genevieve Picard. Additionally, an outside design firm was used to finalize various pieces of the project.

Who ran the project?

The library director and assistant director ran the project.

*What was your objective for the project, and do
you think you achieved that objective?*

The objective of the project was to develop a new identity that would work with the new building. As part of this process, one objective was to integrate the old with the new as much as possible because users had a strong emotional attachment to the original library. The logo did this by using an architectural element from the original building as a key component.

How did you measure success?

There were no specific measures of success. The library wanted to develop a flexible logo that could be used as widely as possible, and that was achieved.

What do you think you did particularly well in this project?

The director felt this project went very well. He and the assistant director were very happy to have been able to work with such a noted illustrator and felt his input made the logo truly outstanding. That feeling was confirmed when the logo won a Massachusetts Library Association PR award.

What do you think could have gone better?

Nothing in particular was identified as needing improvement. The director got the logo he wanted in that it is very flexible, can be adapted for use in various places, and can be used with multiple colors. The library staff has no interest in changing any part of the logo.

Did you get staff involved and, if so, how?

The staff were involved informally. They were shown variations of the logo and asked for their input.

Did you develop brand standards as part of this project? If not, how do you maintain consistency in your branding work?

Brand standards were not developed as part of this project. The library director decided that the logo should be highly flexible and usable with many different colors, so he felt no need to set specific guidelines. The library keeps control of the brand by having materials distributed through the assistant director, who in essence is the brand gatekeeper.

What advice do you have for a library initiating a branding project?

Keep your eyes open—our logo was right here in front of us. Having an open mind and wide open eyes can help you find inspiration in things that you normally take for granted, like architectural elements in your building.

Consider your building's architectural design as a potential source of inspiration.

Consider developing a very adaptable logo—one that can appear in a variety of colors and can be placed in a variety of settings.

Try to make your logo as timeless as possible so it does not have to be redone regularly. Do not use images that can become dated quickly, such as a computer or a mouse.

This logo was fairly conservative because the library's community is fairly conservative. The logo should reflect the nature of the library's community.

Colors for the logo were based on a collection of sea glass that the assistant director had. Again, look around, inspiration can be everywhere!

Harris County Public Library
Houston, Texas
Rhoda Goldberg, Interim Director
Sarah Booth, Marketing Coordinator (former)

Description of project

The entire Harris County Public Library brand manual as described below can be found online at http://data.webjunction.org/wj/documents/14700.pdf.

In 2007, the library's marketing coordinator, Sarah Booth, attended a Public Library Association preconference on branding. She came back to her job determined to develop a branding manual (brand standards) for the Harris County Library system. The system is large, having twenty-six branches all across county. The branches are very community focused but they are also part of one system. The system had a logo, but because it was not used consistently across the various branches, there was a desire for greater consistency.

As one step in the development of its long-range plan, the library had been working on its core values, so that information was available to inform the branding.

All of this work was part of a serious self-evaluation by the system, which had doubled in square footage between 1999 and 2004. It had built two joint-use libraries and two stand-alone libraries and added one branch. The system was growing rapidly and needed to define its direction for the future. Decision makers felt that a branding project would help clarify the community's understanding of the library's role.

Did you see this as a branding project, or did you view it as something else?

The project was started specifically to develop a branding manual and to ensure consistent use of the system's brand (see figure 7).

Who initiated the project and why?

The project was initiated by Sarah Booth, who was the coordinator of marketing and programming. She reported to the deputy director.

Figure 7 Harris County Public Library black-and-white logo

*Who was involved in the project, and what was
each person's relationship to the library?*

The project was managed by the marketing coordinator and the publicity committee and thus involved a variety of library staff. Given the structure of the county government, there was no formal approval system, so staff did not need the consent of any higher authority.

*Who compiled your brand manual? How did you
get funding for the work?*

The manual was both developed and produced in-house. The manual was specifically crafted to be easy to follow, and it was available online.

*What was your objective for the project, and do
you think you achieved that objective?*

The project's objective was to develop a consistent process for using the library's logo so that the system would be seen as having a stronger core identity. There was consistent implementation of the brand standards across the system so the project objective was achieved.

*What was the message that you wanted to convey
with your brand?*

The library wanted the brand to convey who it was as an organization and what made it unique. The brand standards were meant to act as guidelines defining how the brand was to be used to ensure that the library's message was conveyed clearly and consistently. Harris County Public Library is different from Houston Public Library, and there was a need to differentiate.

How did you measure success?

There were no measures for success. The project was deemed successful if staff started using the logo within the parameters of the brand manual.

*What do you think you did particularly well in
this project?*

There was a committee that worked on the project so there was staff buy-in.

The manual ended up being incredibly clear and concise. It made using the logo properly an easy endeavor.

The community colleges that are part of the system had to buy in, and allowing some flexibility in the branding process helped that to happen.

Sarah Booth, the marketing coordinator, owned the project and was passionate about it, so her commitment and enthusiasm powered the project to fruition. Training the staff helped ensure implementation.

What do you think could have gone better?

The project went well, which facilitated the change process. The rationale for making the changes was explained very clearly, and that helped people buy into the concept.

What advice do you have for a library initiating a branding project?

Just do it and do not be afraid of branding. If you want to do it and have a commitment, it will work.

Appoint a brand advocate, someone who is committed to making the project work. Then give her plenty of leeway to get the job done. Look for creative people.

Staff involvement makes a difference in proper execution.

A manager who is supportive helps move the project along.

Words to Describe Your Library and What Makes It Unique

This list is intended to serve as a starting point for your Core Team members as they work to identify key terms that describe your library and what makes it unique. Those terms will then lead to your brand tagline. Please see chapter 6 for full instructions on how to use this list.

abstract
accessible
beautiful
beneficial
better than Borders
books
boring
brotherhood
busy
careful
caring
casual
chaotic
cheap
clan
classical
clean
clique
closeness
club
colorful
combination

comfortable
complex
complicated
comprehensive
concerned
conservative
continuity
cool
cooperation
cost-effective
creative
credible
crowded
customer-oriented
difficult
diverse
dull
easy
educational
elegant
energized
engaged

enjoyable
evolutionary
evolving
exciting
experienced
fit in
formal
friendly
full
fun
genuine
hands-on
hangout
hard to understand
hip
inexpensive
intelligent
interesting
intimidating
isolated
junction
kinship

literal
local
minimal
modern
network
nexus
noisy
old
ordinary
pace-setting
partner
partnership
pioneering
plain
premium
professional

refuge
regional
relationship oriented
responsive
rich
robust
rowdy
rural
safe
savvy
scary
simple
sisterhood
sleek
soothing
strategic

stunning
superficial
tactical
tolerant
traditional
tried-and-true
unfriendly
urban
useful
valuable
valued
warm
welcoming
wise
young

Glossary

■ ■ ■ ■ ■ ■ ■ ■ ■ ■ ■ ■ ■

This glossary provides definitions of various branding and marketing terms that can be found in this book. They are not meant to be official definitions but rather simple explanations of terms that can be very confusing. The number that follows each definition indicates the chapter in which the related topic is explored.

Absolutes. Work that must or must not happen as part of a brand logo design project. (7)

Advertising. The action of talking directly to possible users of your product to tell them how that product can fulfill a need in their lives. (1)

Attribute branding. A brand that tells its story in terms of the specific details that make a product or service look or act a certain way, such as its color or shape or speed. (2)

Audit. A review of your brand as it is today so that you can determine where it exists on a continuum of development. Once you understand where your brand is today, you can determine your next steps to move forward. (5)

Blog. A user-generated website where writers put their thoughts down and readers can respond. Combination of *web* and *log*—blog. (12)

Brand advocate. The person who oversees how a brand is being developed and is used in a library. The person who identifies situations in which the brand is not being used appropriately or with consistency and also identifies potentially positive evolutions of the brand that the library might want to adopt. (8)

Brand look. Also known as *brand identity*. The visual representation of the library and its story. The look is seen in the library's logo, its colors, specific lettering that might be used in written publications, pictures of the library building, library cards, name tags worn by staff—any visual representation of the library and its services. (1)

Brand message. An internal statement meant to identify the library's role to its public in terms that are meaningful and relevant to that public. (6)

Brand standards. A formal set of guidelines for the brand. Standards come in two forms—editorial and design. Editorial standards provide guidelines for writing about that brand. Design standards give guidelines for how to use the visual components of the brand, such as the logo and brand colors. (8)

Branding. A component of the marketing process that defines who you want to talk to about your product or service, articulates a clear message about what makes your product unique and meaningful, and then conveys that information in a method that captures the attention of potential customers and encourages them to act. (1)

Buzz. When one person tells another person about a product or service. (6)

Case statement. An articulation of the justification for the branding project. It provides the following information: a summary of the specific activities that make up the branding project; a definition of the project's objective; a specific, detailed description of what is expected of individuals who become involved in the project (three meetings lasting two hours each, reading of four documents, etc.); and why the project is important for the library. (3)

Checkpoint Team. A group of individuals who should be brought into the branding process at key checkpoints. (3)

Consideration set. A shortcut for figuring out the best choice based on previously discovered information. Because people seeking information cannot possibly go through all available sources, they develop consideration sets. They begin by researching and trying out many different brands that might fulfill a specific need (like the need for information) and end by narrowing down their choices to several brands that actually could meet their needs. Then, when they have the same need in the future, they can avoid going back and researching all their options again. They have developed a set of brands (a consideration set) that they know will work, and they limit their consideration to those brands. (2)

Core Team. A group of individuals who absolutely must be involved in the branding process from beginning to end. (3)

Creative brief. A statement written by the brand project manager that identifies all key elements a designer must know before starting to design a brand logo. (7)

Deliverables. The actual things that you should have in hand at the end of a project such as reports and designs. (7)

Demographic segmenting. Identifying fairly large groups of potential users by demographic factors such as age, gender, income, or geographic location. (1)

Emotional branding. A brand that tells its story in terms of how it can fulfill some esoteric need that a user has. Such brand stories tend to appeal more to the emotion and less to the intellect of a potential user. (2)

Great brand. A product or service that consumers remember clearly and is part of their ongoing thought process or consideration set. (4)

Honest brand. A brand that delivers what it says it will deliver. It does not make overblown promises, such as "Use this toothpaste and you will become rich and sexy." (4)

Library story. The articulation of the role a library plays or wants to play in its community. (2)

Marketing. The process of (a) developing a story about a product or service that explains what makes it unique and why potential users will find it interesting, (b) identifying the potential audience to whom this story should be told, and (c) developing ways of telling the story in an intriguing and attention-getting way. (1)

Marketing plan. A document that identifies, across the period of a year, what library activities will need some sort of promotion. (8)

Marketing strategy. The first part of the marketing process: identifying who will hear the library's story and then developing the story. It is planning that is done before any actual marketing is put into motion. It is a strategy because it defines a series of plans developed to achieve a specific goal. (1)

Mission statement. An articulation of why an organization exists, including its goals, aspirations, and values. It is generally an internal, strategic document meant to act as a guidepost that tells an organization how it should operate. (6)

Objectives. The identification of what you want to have happen because of the entire marketing process. (1)

Portfolio. A compilation of an artist's work. (7)

Promotion. Any activity that an organization engages in to develop awareness about a specific activity. (1)

Public relations. Any activity that results in a third-party mention of your product or service. (1)

Sales. The process of matching a buyer to the product or service that he wants to buy. (1)

Segmenting. Identifying the total universe of individuals who might use your product and then breaking that universe into smaller segments that you can study to understand if they might be interested in your product. (1)

Support Team. The group of individuals who need general information about the progress of the branding project but probably only at the beginning, middle, and end of the work. (3)

Tactical marketing. The second part of the marketing process: developing and implementing tools to tell the story in a compelling manner. Actions taken to promote a product in the marketplace. (1)

Tagline. A short, intriguing, and attention-grabbing statement based on the branding message that is intended to appeal to potential users of the library. (6)

Target audience. A specific group of people that the library wants to hear and respond to the branding message. (1)

Template. A sample product (such as a bookmark) that holds certain design elements constant but allows the content and certain other components (such as colors) to be changed to fit the needs of specific events. (8)

Vision statement. A statement that defines a library's desired role in the future. (6)

Acknowledgments

I would like to acknowledge the following two individuals for playing very important roles in training me to be a librarian and teaching me to be a leader:

Bob Dugan, one of my Simmons College professors, who was always very supportive of a businessperson becoming a librarian

Sharon Gilley, my first library director, who was always encouraging and willing to try my ideas

Index

■ ■ ■ ■ ■ ■ ■ ■ ■ ■ ■ ■ ■ ■

Note: Page numbers in italics indicate definitions.

logos (cont.)
>   vs. tagline, 44
>   uses of, 29
>   variations of as deliverables, 53
>   *See also* brand look; visual identity of brand

Lucius Beebe Memorial Library
>   (Wakefield, Mass.)
>   case study, 100–103
>   design standards, 60–61
>   editorial guidelines, 59–60
>   logo and tagline, 5, 45, 54
>   overview, ix
>   staff involvement, 23

M

market research, 6
marketing, *1*, *115*
marketing plan, 63–64, *115*
marketing process, 8–9
marketing strategy, 2–6, 8, *115*
marketing tactics. *See* tactical marketing
marketing tools in marketing plan, 64
Maxwell House Coffee brand, 28
meetings and brand audit, 32–33
message of brand, 25–27, 38–49, *114*
>   attribute or emotion, 43–44
>   in brand audit, 32–36
>   and community, 39–40
>   in creative brief, 54
>   delivering on, 83
>   evaluation of, 39
>   importance of, 94, 95
>   and mission of library, 40–43
>   and non-memorable logos/taglines, 46
>   strength, 77
>   tagline, 44–46, 48–49

mission statement, *115*
>   vs. brand, ix
>   and brand message, 40–42
>   developing brand message without a
>   mission, 42–43
>   importance of, 96

must-have features (absolutes), 54, *113*

N

new users as target audience, 3, 5
Nike brand logo, 4, 27
non-users and defining role of the library, 17

O

objectives in creative brief, 53
objectives in marketing strategy, 2–3, 8, 79, *115*
online work spaces, use of, 10
opposition to branding process, 17

P

parking as part of brand, 5
participants in branding process, 16–24
>   identification of, 16–18
>   team creation, 18–20
>   team roles, 20–21
>   *See also* Core Team

"Pass It on Week" promotion, 47
patrons. *See* users
perfection, hazards of, 71
planning, importance of, 96
political considerations, 17, 21
portfolios, evaluation of, 52, *115*
print-ready logo, 54
printing of materials, 52, 57
prior brand. *See* brands, prior
pro bono work and consultants, 51, 67
project leader, characteristics of, 19, 23, 94–95
project plan, sample, xii–xiii
promotion, 7, *115*
>   of blog, 90–91

proposals from consultants, 69
public relations, 7, *115*

Q

quantifiable objectives, 3, 79. *See also* objectives in creative brief; objectives in marketing strategy; statistics on use
quiet place, library as, 14, 44

R

reading about marketing, 72
references from consultants and designers, 52, 69–70, 72
relationships, importance of, 73
>   exercise, 74

repetition of brand, 28, 36
role of library
>   and consumers' consideration sets, 13–14
>   and selection of team members, 17
>   as story, 4